Altered Books Workshop

18 creative techniques for self-expression

Bev Brazelton

NORTH LIGHT BOOKS
CINCINNATI, OHIO
www.artistsnetwork.com

About the Author

Bev Brazelton has been studying and making art for most of her adult life. She has sold her art in a variety of venues and is currently teaching altered books, bookmaking and paper arts classes and workshops around the country. She finds that her loves of art, teaching and traveling combine into a lifestyle that suits her perfectly. She currently lives on the central coast of California with her husband and two cats.

Altered Books Workshop: 18 Creative Techniques for Self-Expression.
Copyright © 2004 by Bev Brazelton. Manufactured in China. All rights reserved. No part of this book may be reproduced in any form or by any electronic or mechanical means including information storage and retrieval systems without permission in writing from the publisher, except by a reviewer who may quote brief passages in a review. Published by North Light Books, an imprint of F+W Publications, Inc., 4700 East Galbraith Road, Cincinnati, Ohio, 45236. (800) 289-0963. First Edition.

Other fine North Light Books are available from your local bookstore, art supply store or direct from the publisher.

08 07 06 05 04   5 4 3 2 1

Library of Congress Cataloging-in-Publication Data
Brazelton, Bev
    Altered books workshop : 18 creative techniques for self-expression /
Bev Brazelton.
        p. cm
    Includes index.
    ISBN 1-58180-535-7 (pbk. : alk. paper)
    1. Altered books. I. Title.

TT896.3.B73 2004
702'.8'1—dc22

                                          2003059396

Editor: Amanda Metcalf
Designer: Stephanie Strang
Production Artist: Donna Cozatchy
Production Coordinator: Sara Dumford
Photographers: Tim Grondin, Al Parrish and Christine Polomsky
Photo Stylist: Jan Nickum

metric conversion chart		
To Convert	To	Multiply By
Inches	Centimeters	2.54
Centimeters	Inches	0.4
Feet	Centimeters	30.5
Centimeters	Feet	0.03
Yards	Meters	0.9
Meters	Yards	1.1
Sq. Inches	Sq. Centimeters	6.45
Sq. Centimeters	Sq. Inches	0.16
Sq. Feet	Sq. Meters	0.09
Sq. Meters	Sq. Feet	10.8
Sq. Yards	Sq. Meters	0.8
Sq. Meters	Sq. Yards	1.2
Pounds	Kilograms	0.45
Kilograms	Pounds	2.2
Ounces	Grams	28.3
Grams	Ounces	0.035

Dedication

This book is dedicated to my amazing family: Jennifer, Tom, Monica, Greg, little Ruby and especially my husband, Dan, who has been my partner and a patron of my art for many years.

Acknowledgments

Thank you, F+W Publications, for publishing this book. A special thanks to Tricia Waddell for a great start, to my editor Amanda Metcalf for her energy and patience, and to the very talented photographer Christine Polomsky. You have all made this such a wonderful experience.

I also would like to thank MaryJo McGraw and Connie Williams for their support and for recommending me to North Light Books, and Mary Jines for her generosity. Thanks also to my students for sharing their support and artistic spirits.

Contents

chapter three

Intermediate Techniques

Add a touch of class with paint and three-dimensional effects.

60

chapter four

Creative Techniques

Wow anyone and everyone with something a little out of the box.

88

Introduction

I altered my first book in 1990, after a trip to China. While touring, I took tons of pictures and then incorporated them into a used book of Chinese writing that I had found. I didn't know at the time that what I was doing would become the huge craft trend that it is today.

I like the idea of altering books, of recycling old ones and transforming them into something entirely new. For me, altering a book is a form of journaling. I find that every page represents where I am in my life and in my artistic process. Even if I'm not deliberately communicating a message, the images, papers and writing I choose always are connected in some way to what is currently happening in my life.

It's exciting to constantly experiment with new ideas and materials. And it's low pressure: If I mess up, I just rip out the page. I find satisfaction in the idea that I can work out an entire theme or feeling within the framework of a book. Their size and portability make altered books an art form I can work on anywhere I go. I teach altered book classes around the country and always enjoy watching students get excited and inspired by this art form.

If you've dabbled in altered books before, I hope this book inspires you to try new materials and ideas and to incorporate them into your work. If you've never tried it before, I hope this book inspires your entry to a whole other world.

Enjoy!

Next Page: The collage on pages 8 and 9 lets the words of the book show through the paint, inviting you to study all the different layers. The pennies, while not large, add that tiny bit of three-dimensionality that challenges a mind used to looking at a two-dimensional book.

been luck... to... gender
happy to b... ...ked m...
...even wa...

de...
...
us...
m...
do...
can...
ba... ...ay... of a man...
most of whom label the...
living proof tha...
...hap the...

upsets me that most women can't do... it if
has a f...

· · · · · chapter **one** · · · ·

Getting Started

Congratulations! You're about to begin a fantastic journey into the world of altered books. This chapter will list tools and materials you'll need to get started. These aren't the only tools or materials around—you can use just about anything to alter a book—but they'll get you going. The rest is up to your imagination.

Before you begin altering, you'll need to choose a book—think about the age of the book, the size, the title, the content or even the feel of the pages—and whether you want a theme. Maybe you don't care and you just want to jump in and see what happens. Just do what you feel.

Take a glance at these pages to learn about materials, book options, themes and how to progress through an altered page. Altering books isn't an exact science by any means, but it is an art, and the basic knowledge in these pages will help you enjoy it even more.

What Is an Altered Book?

The altered book is an art form in which artists recycle or transform existing books into new works of art. The book, an artwork in itself, becomes a canvas for new ideas and images. Altered books are a rapidly growing part of the craft world, but they're actually an old method of recycling. In the eleventh century, Italian monks recycled old vellum manuscripts by scraping off the ink and adding new text and illustrations to the blank pages to create a new book. Called Palimpsest, the process often left parts of the old text visible through the new. These monks were creating new books, new pieces of art, on old ones.

Altered book artists do the same, though the techniques usually yield more colorful, visual results. Today, we alter books by removing pages; adding new pages, photographs, letters, cards and other inserts; tearing,

A Scrapbook or Journal

My altered books don't usually follow themes unless an event really affects me. I created an altered book called "The Fall" about a time I fell off the porch while taking a photo. I preserved the experience through a busy collection of black and white and obvious and abstract images and collages of cameras, eyes, reclining figures, black mesh and other embellishments. The book tells the story from aiming the camera, through my fall, my ailing time and my recovery. "The Fall" is an altered book and a journal about that experience.

A Practice Book

I always recommend that altered book artists and students keep a practice book, just as painters keep scrap paper to try out new techniques or preview a color combination. Of course, if you mess up in an altered book, you can always just rip out the pages, but it's helpful to master a technique or try out different colors before you work in an official altered book. And of course, the practice book can serve as its own journal of your artistic experiences and progress as you learn the craft.

cutting, gluing, stitching and painting pages; and any-thing else you can think of. You can let the original content of the book play as little or big a part of your new artwork as you want, letting words or images show through or covering them up to use the book's pages simply as a surface.

You can develop compositions and themes or you can follow your gut. You can work on each page or spread sepa-rately, or you can work on the whole book as a greater piece of artwork. You can create altered books to serve as journals, scrapbooks, gifts, keepsakes, artists' sketchbooks, commissioned artworks or just because you feel like it. You can do what you want and say what you want; if you're altering it, you're creating an altered book!

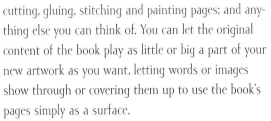

A Book You Do Just Because

I'm lucky enough to have a studio filled with altered books, supplies and other artwork—journals and hand-made books. I work in books constantly, and I couldn't possibly be expected to have an intended purpose for each one. Mostly I just work on what I want to work on when I feel like working on it. What results is not a conscious attempt at a mes-sage, theme or statement, but it's a reflection of me, my moods and my thoughts nonetheless. My advice is to just open up a book and start working. Don't worry about the deeper questions of what and why. It's all art-work in the end.

Tools and Materials

The craft of altered books can use a lot of materials, though it doesn't require them. You can use embellishments, collage materials, paints and glazes, or you can use none of these. Altered books literally are what you make of them.

On the following pages are plenty of materials you can use to alter books, but don't let this list stand in your way. All you really absolutely need to get started is a bit of glue and the contents of your junk drawer. See what you can do. You might surprise yourself!

General Materials

I always keep several pairs of scissors on my work table for cutting different materials. To make sure they stay sharp, I keep one pair of small scissors just for cutting small pieces of paper or fine details.

Although I'm not overly concerned with neat pages and straight lines, they're sometimes necessary, so keep a pencil and ruler nearby. Use a craft knife to cut through pages. Place a cutting mat behind the page or pages you're cutting to protect your work surface and the other pages of your book.

Paints and Glazes

When working with paints, which cover the surface more fully than glazes do, I use only acrylic-based paints and materials. Acrylics are less toxic than oils and they dry quickly, which helps when I'm too excited about my work to wait. I also love that I can mix any acrylic with other paint brands to create the effects I'm seeking for a page design.

Use glazes when you want to see the layers or surface underneath. I'm completely hooked on glazes. Apply one or a few and you can see the text or elements beneath, or layer more glazes to add sophistication to your pages. You can buy premixed glazes or make your own by mixing any acrylic paint with a glazing medium.

Paintbrushes

I use flat paintbrushes between sizes 8 and 14. Flat brushes look like miniature house-painting brushes with a thin rectangular group of hairs. You'll use these brushes to apply paints, glazes and glue. Use professional-quality brushes to apply paint; it makes a big difference in the finished piece. Use cheaper brushes to apply glue because cleaning it out of brushes can be a challenge. Foam brushes, which are less expensive and disposable, also work well for applying glue. I have one other brush in my collection, a stipple brush, which produces wonderful textures when dabbed on the page to lift or apply paints or glazes, as on page 72.

Heat Gun

You can use a heat gun or hair dryer to speed up the drying time of paint, but be careful. The heat doesn't work with every technique, such as image transfers, so read the instructions for each technique first.

FLAT BRUSHES

STIPPLE BRUSH

PVA Glue

PVA is an archival, fast-drying glue that I like to use for papers and other light objects. I use it all the time—so much, in fact, that I buy it by the gallon. It's a great glue for bookmaking. However, because it sets quickly, you can't reposition images or objects once they're in place.

E6000

To adhere heavy embellishments or those I'm placing in fragile areas, I use E6000. I don't use it as often as PVA, but I always keep at least one tube in my studio. Beware that some people are sensitive to its smell.

Gel Medium

Acrylic paint gel medium is an ideal adhesive for altered books. It dries clear, so you can use it as a heavy glue for embellishments or for papers of any weight. When I'm working on an altered book, I generally grab whatever is closest, so I often use gel medium and PVA interchangeably. If you've never tried gel medium before, give it a shot.

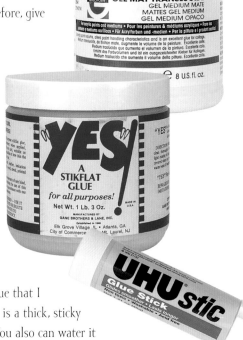

Tape

Sometimes tape is just plain easier to work with than glue. I use it to secure pages in place when doing a folding technique or to attach inserts or tags. You also can apply double-stick tape straight to the book page and attach an insert or even fibers directly over it. Use plain Scotch tape to attach items when the tape won't be visible.

Other Adhesives

Perfect Paper Adhesive (PPA) is a nonsticky glue that I like to use for gluing light weight papers. YES is a thick, sticky glue that you can apply with a palette knife. You also can water it down and apply it with a brush. It's a good all-purpose adhesive, but if you're a messy gluer like I am, you might not like YES glue very much. When working away from my studio, I use glue sticks because they're portable and don't spill.

Rubber Stamping Materials

Rubber stamping is a wonderful way to add an accent or focal point to your page. You can use a stamp as a background or as the final touch that brings the page together. You can stamp directly on the page or on collage images and inserts, such as tags, before attaching them to your book. I don't use one special type of ink exclusively. Instead, I'm always experimenting with different brands and kinds. It keeps the style and look of my books fresh, and sometimes I stumble upon a great product, color or mixture of colors.

Hole Punches

Decorate tags, cards and other inserts with interesting hole punches, or thread embellishments or fibers through punched holes. You can even use a large hole punch to create an opening for a window and use acetate or mesh as the window's "glass." Then simply place an image or word behind it for a unique perspective.

To use a Japanese screw punch, place a cutting mat behind the page or pages you're punching, and just press down. You don't have to position it around both sides of the page as with a normal hole punch. This lets you be more exact with your "aim."

JAPANESE SCREW PUNCH

Texturing Materials

Plastic wrap, wax paper, aluminum foil, tissue paper and anything else you can crumple all make interesting marks in wet paint. You also can place wax paper between closed pages while they dry to create a consistent texture across the entire page. Dab dry sponges over wet paint to lift paint up, or make imprints with sponges loaded with paint. Paper towels also are handy for lifting paint when you applied too much or want to lighten an area.

Post-It Labeling and Cover-Up Tape

Post-It tape is a thin masking tape that lets you cover words, lines of text or areas of a page to protect them from paint or rubber stamps.

Collage Papers

Collage papers are abundant nowadays; you can find them in almost any craft, art supply or specialty paper store. I'm an impulse buyer when it comes to paper, believing that certain papers simply call my name as I walk past. So go explore the wonderful word of speciality papers and find the ones that call out to you. These are the ones that will work best for your personal style of artistic expression.

Collage Images

The altered pages featured in this book are made of composite material, as your pages will be. Look for collage images anywhere you can think of, including magazines, books, postcards, old calendars and even junk mail. I like the vintage look and find lots of old materials in antique stores and other old books. Find the

images and materials that appeal to you. Put these materials together in your altered books and your art truly will be your own.

Three-Dimensional Embellishments

Almost any embellishment can go in an altered book. The only thing that limits what you can do is the thickness of the embellishments you collect: Your book doesn't need to lie completely flat when you finish, but it should at least close. Of course, if you just can't turn away from a large embellishment, you can cut a shadowbox to hold it (see page 62).

Keep an eye out for buttons, puzzle pieces, charms, game pieces, old jewelry and coins. Look at garage sales, flea markets, antique stores, thrift stores and in your own home. Check the junk drawer and your jewelry box. Those items you never wanted to throw out but don't know what to do with can be immortalized in your altered book. You could even make a junk drawer-themed book!

Fibers and Beads

I like to use fibers as accents to my pages. I often lay collections of different fibers along the spine between two pages. Even when a book is closed, fibers hang over the edges and really emphasize the three-dimensional nature of altered books. Look in craft and fabric stores. There's a huge selection out there!

Glue beads to your pages as decoration, use them as drawer handles (see page 94), or hang them from fibers. For a fun twist, try creating a necklace or earrings out of beads and putting them on a picture of a woman—or a man for that matter!

Eyelet Tools

Eyelets are a popular way to attach and hang embellishments. You'll need an eyelet setter and a hammer to use them (see pages 101 and 102). You also can use fibers and a dental floss threader or wire and needlenose pliers to attach embellishments.

EYELETS

CRAFT HAMMER

EYELET SETTER

NEEDLENOSE PLIERS

DENTAL FLOSS THREADER

WIRE

Choosing a Book

really like the idea of recycling old books, so I look for used books to alter. The best places I have found for good used books are thrift stores, garage sales, flea markets and used book stores. Sometimes I check my own book shelves to see what pops out at me.

I almost always work with hardback books because they seem sturdier and more likely to stand up to the altering process as well as the passage of time. Then I alter paperbacks when I feel like doing something a bit different.

Do You Like the Feel?

I also choose a book by how it feels. I avoid books with pages that feel thin because I like pages strong enough to stand up to whatever I may decide to do. I also prefer pages that aren't glossy. But remember that these are my personal choices, not rules, and your preferences may be different. Go with the book that feels right to you. You'll enhance your creative expression if you love the feel of the book you're working on. I sometimes like working on children's books that have thick pages, more like board than paper. They make the altered book seem much sturdier and provide a unique feel.

Do You Like the Size?

I choose a book for a number of reasons. The first consideration is the size of the book. For your first altering experience, I recommend a medium-sized hardback book, but no book is out of the question as an altering opportunity. I work on books of several different sizes at a time because I find that one doesn't always fit my mood.

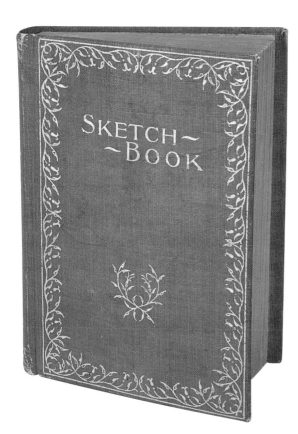

Is It in Good Condition?

Another consideration when choosing a book to alter is its age. The pages of older books are brittle, making working with them a challenge. One of the first books I altered was published in 1902. I loved the title and illustration on the cover, but after altering a few pages, the book started to fall apart and I gave up. I don't want you to have this experience for your first try. Don't work on a book older than one hundred years old, and use your judgement on anything else.

If you're absolutely in love with an old book, use the cover or pages as materials to alter another book. The book at left, a revised edition of *Sketch Book* by Washington Irving, was published in 1848. The pages are a brownish yellow and too soft to work with. But I love the cover. I plan to remove the pages and make another book within these covers. Then I can use the rest of the pages anywhere in any of my altered books.

Does Something About It Just Catch Your Eye?

Sometimes, a title catches my interest and sparks ideas for the altering process. Other times I buy books just because I like the covers. If the cover fits in with the theme of another book, I might photocopy it or remove it and use it there.

Developing a Theme

An altered book's theme can chronicle an experience, as shown in these altered pages. It also can feature a color scheme, a historical event, a person you love or admire (or perhaps don't like much at all), a favorite hobby, favorite type of music, a favorite altering technique, etc.

Most often, though, I don't really work on a book with a specific theme in mind. I simply work in several books at a time. When the mood strikes, I go to my studio and just do what comes naturally. If the colors in a book that I've already begun strike me, I might alter more pages in that book with a similar color scheme or maybe even a contrasting one. Sometimes I feel like working with certain materials, like paints or fibers. Sometimes I feel like doing a certain technique, like folding pages or stitching.

If the size of a book I've begun catches my eye, I'll work there. Working in this manner, you might notice that some of your books have developed themes without effort on your part. In all of your altered books, though, the strongest theme simply will be that the art speaks to you.

The Fall

I created this book, which I call "The Fall," after I fell off my front porch while photographing my artwork. I took a step backward to get a better shot and stepped right off the porch. I hurt my hip and needed a trip to the doctor and X-rays. Everything turned out fine, but over a month passed before it stopped hurting. I found myself feeling angry, so I decided to release my feelings into this book.

In my collection of books to be altered, I found a photography instruction book. Because I had fallen while taking photographs, I thought this was the perfect starting point. (I wonder if this photography book instructed readers to look behind them before stepping back!) I started by painting the entire book inside and out with black paint to establish a common element throughout the book. With white and gray elements added, the black-and-white scheme resembles old camera film and photos and creates a stark, tense feeling that matched the feelings I was experiencing as I worked.

(1) The Cover

I usually do the cover of a book last. I loved this black-and-white image because of the horror on the viewer's faces. It's the expression I would have imagined on people's faces if they had seen me fall. The black-and-white image fits my color scheme, and the people in the image are looking through 3-D glasses, similar to me looking through the camera's viewfinder when I fell.

Next, I added several images from an old art history book. Most of them had an eerie or intimidating feel, which contributed to the dark tone of the book. Included were images of sculptures of reclining figures, which represent me stuck in bed or on the couch during my recovery. Sure, being bedridden doesn't sound so bad sometimes, but I was desperate to be up and about and working on my artwork, among other things.

Then, I added collage papers, rubber stamped images and embellishments, all the while staying with the black-and-white scheme. All of these elements came together to form an abstract, chaotic design. The out-of-control feel of the book certainly represents how I felt both about falling and about lying in recovery.

I created the entire book in one day. It was one of those pieces of art that just fell onto the pages as fast as I could work. When all was said and done, though, at least I ended up with a good story and a great book!

(2) Looking Through the Camera

This page seems whimsical. At this point in my story, I was still in a good mood, out on the porch on a nice day working on some photography. The wiggle eyes represent that all of my attention was focused through the camera. For all the fun this page includes, the illegible scribbling still holds a sense of foreboding.

(3) Falling

With one too many steps backward, confusion set in as I took a tumble off the porch. Notice the downward movement of the eyeballs, the shocked and miserable expression on the figure in the center and the black mesh that obscures an already confusing scene.

(4) In Pain

Although this page seems a bit calmer than the previous one, the weight of the black indicates that I'm still not in a wonderful mood. The reclining figure looks sick, tired and in pain. At this point, things aren't moving as fast as during the fall, but the slowness and stillness is just as torturous.

The General Process

lthough it's fun just to let things happen when altering books, some thinking ahead is necessary. You need to start your book differently if you're adding inserts or cutting shadowboxes, niches or drawers. You'll start most altered books by ripping out some of the original pages, which will make room to add elements, such as inserts. Shadowboxes, niches and drawers use a continuous block of pages, though, so you'll need to plan such techniques and remember not to remove any pages. Below is the general process I follow as I work on a book or page.

Choose Your Book
Look at pages 20 and 21 for information on how to choose a book. Or just pick one up and let's get started!

Rip Out Pages
You'll add so many materials as you alter the book that you'll need to remove pages to make sure it closes. Even paint adds thickness. Just open the book to a page near the front and rip out a few pages. Work your way to the back of the book, removing pages every so often. If you want the pages in the binding to be even, remove pages at consistent intervals. Or just rip them whenever and wherever you feel like it. And, of course, you can always rip out more pages later.

See the Difference?
Compare the thickness of the book before and after I removed pages. It makes a big difference. It looks empty, but I can guarantee that when I finish this book, it will be plenty full.

Don't Be Intimidated

I find that the hardest part of starting a new book is just that—to start.

Add Color

To avoid thinking about what to do first, simply add color to two or three pages with the same paint. Use a heat gun or blow dryer to dry the paint, or just put a sheet of wax paper between wet pages to keep them from sticking together. Then close the pages together and continue painting other pages. Sometimes I go through an entire book just adding color all over the place before doing anything else. When you finish painting, remove all of the wax paper and prop up the book to let the pages dry.

Add Collage Images

Once the pages are dry, glue whatever collage images and paper you like to a page. I like to use a full two-page spread as one canvas. I think it adds to the continuity and flow of the finished work.

Take a Step Back

Every once in a while, look at your page as a whole. This page needed another element, another punch of color, so I've added the flower bursts.

Add More Color
I like to use layers in my artwork, whether of glazes, collage images, collage papers or all of them. Here I added a thin, green glaze.

Add More Collage Materials
Any more materials you add won't have the color of the previous glazes, though they will take on future glazes.

Add Another Glaze
Are you getting the picture yet? I added another green glaze, so the layers with two glazes look a bit more green while the color on the newer collage layers is more subtle.

Pull It Together

As before, take a step back and look at the entire page. I like the reddish flowers I added earlier, but the one on the right just doesn't look right to me, so I've removed it. Notice the color of the original yellow showing through where I removed the collage image. Though you can mask areas or shapes as part of a planned technique, that wasn't my intention here, so I added another glaze to keep the yellow spot from standing out too much. Metallic glazes are always a nice way to finish a page with a touch of sophistication.

Add Embellishments

After all the glue and glazes have dried, add embellishments any way you'd like. Fibers add so much texture to a page. The gold ornaments hanging off the fibers are a pair of gypsy-like earrings my editor received as a gift on a trip to Russia. Can't you just feel the fibers and hear the charms jingling together?

Add Finishing Touches

Because I removed the flower from the right side, I need to add something else to balance the pages. I took apart the second earring and glued three of the charms onto each page. Then I framed the figure's face with a matching gold embellishment.

Just keep working until your pages come together. You'll know when you're done. If you're not sure, put the book aside. You might come up with another idea later, or maybe at second glance you'll realize you like it as is.

... listening for familiar footsteps in the long hospital
corridor or waiting for the sound of a car stopping outside your
house ... you have had ... you will also remem-
ber how one caller ... spirit and ... another,
whose intentions w... away leaving you
... the difference?
From the point ... ors can be a help
or a hindrance. Th... he patient as they
would like to be ... mstances, but the
inexperienced or the ... eceive how it feels to

· · · · · · · · · chapter two · · ·

Basic Techniques

Now that you've chosen your book and have your supplies ready, let's begin. The techniques in this chapter are simple, so your first steps into altering books will be easy ones. Basic collage skills are very helpful when altering books and can be used on a page with almost any other technique. So start by simply adding some images and papers to a few pages. All of a sudden, you'll have gone from blank pages to artistic statements. You can leave collaged pages as they are for simple statements, or you can continue working on the pages with other techniques.

Stitching is one way to add interest and texture to a page. Or you can cut doors to make your page interactive, drawing the observer into the page. Windows allow the observer to peek through a page and see images or words on the next one, a glimpse into the future. Adding tags is a simple way to create "new pages" different in look and dimension from the rest. There are a variety of ways to add them. Folding pages easily changes the appearance of a page. Folded pockets can hold tags, messages and cards.

Simply put, the techniques in this chapter provide easy ways to dramatically alter the appearance of your pages. Plus, they're guaranteed to get your own creativity flowing.

believe

Collaging

Collage is an art form in which bits of papers, images and embellishments are pasted onto a surface. The trick to collage is layering. You can layer by adding paints, inks, images, papers and three-dimensional objects. The more layers, the more sophisticated your collage will be. Here, you'll get started by adding images and papers to your book. As this book progresses, we'll build on this basic technique.

✂ MATERIALS 2 pages of your book; collage images; collage papers; flat paintbrush; PVA glue; yellow ochre glaze; wax paper

1 ADD A GLAZE • Apply a layer of glaze over the two-page spread.

2 CREATE TEXTURE • Before the glaze dries, place a sheet of wax paper between the pages, close the pages together, and lightly run your hand over the back of each page. This is an easy way to add texture. Remove the wax paper and leave the book open until the pages dry.

3 ADD COLLAGE IMAGES • Apple glue to the back of an image with a flat brush. Place the image on the page and smooth it out with your hand to remove wrinkles and bubbles.

4 ADD COLLAGE PAPER • Add pieces of paper to your collage the same way, paying attention to your composition.

5 FIND A PLEASING DESIGN • Continue adding collage papers until you have a composition that pleases you. There really is no wrong way to do collage. Just keep experimenting until you find your style.

TIP! Tearing collage papers and images can give a softer edge to the overall look of the page.

Variations

RIGHT: I pulled a warm color scheme from the girl's coat in the image at right, toning it down a bit to warm pinks and purples. The black fibers add a strong color impact and imitate the complex layers of rubber stamped text. A pastel purple textured collage paper provides a subtle contrast to the more intense colors on the rest of the page.

BELOW: There's a lot more going on here than at first glance. The large image and buttons add interest, but underneath them, some of the original page's text shows through, a few magazine clippings show a bit more text, and collage paper with a script pattern covers most of the page. On top of that, a white, textured collage paper is glazed with a reddish brown that complements the woman's hair. Yellow paper around the face and buttons brings out the yellow in her skin tone.

ABOVE: Here I used just two large images. Even the silhouette on the left isn't obvious at first. The rest of the collage uses solid-colored, textured collage papers and glazes.

LEFT: This is a more organized collage, using symmetrical images. The lettering on the left and the figures on the right are also symmetrical, at least in general shape. The fibers, beads and embellishments hanging off the edges of other pages in the book provide a bit of texture and interest to this very balanced page.

Stitching

Stitching is a fun, easy way to add interest to altered pages. There are many ways to stitch a page—using an assortment of fibers, threads and ribbons; stitching pages together to form pockets; framing the page or an image—you're limited only by your imagination.

You'll need four two-sided pages of your altered book for this technique. I'll refer to these as pages 1-4, referring to the front of page 2 or the back of page 4, for example.

✂ MATERIALS 4 pages of your book; dental floss threader; fibers; hole punch; scissors

1 FOLD THE CORNERS • Paint all four pages. Open to the back of page 1 and the front of page 2. Fold the top corner of page 2 toward page 1, bringing the fold all the way to the spine. Fold the back of page 3 toward the front of page 4 the same way.

2 PUNCH HOLES • Holding pages 1 and 2 together, punch holes on the side of the pages from the fold down to the bottom and along the bottom to the spine. Hold pages 3 and 4 together and punch holes the same way.

3 THREAD FIBER THROUGH THE HOLE • Cut a length of fiber approximately twice the width of the book. Holding pages 1 and 2 together, thread the fiber up through the bottom of the first hole. Leave 3 to 4 inches (8 to 10 centimeters) of thread to hang off the edge of the book. Tie a knot to hold it in place.

4 CREATE STITCHES • Wrap the fiber around the edge of the page and thread it through the next hole. When you reach the spine, thread the fiber across the spine and continue threading through the holes in pages 3 and 4. Make sure you thread through both pages on this side as well.

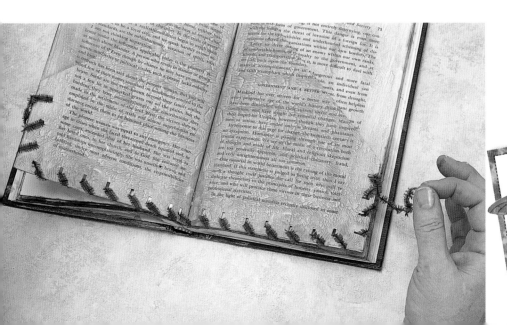

5 TIE THE END • When you've reached the last hole, tie a knot in the fiber and trim it to the same length as the other end. You can insert anything into the pockets you've just created.

TIP! For threading the fibers, use a plastic dental floss threader. You can find them in clear plastic cases of about twenty-four next to the dental floss and toothbrushes in any drug store. Floss threaders are wonderful for stitching and beading because they are flexible and can fit through any embellishment or hole.

Variations

RIGHT: I often use double-stick tape to adhere folded pages to other pages to make pockets, but here I used gold stitching. The stitches and beads add an Oriental feel, also indicated by the Chinese brush painting-like brushstrokes. Notice that although you can see the text through the light blue glaze, it doesn't interfere with or detract from the design.

BELOW: Stitching also is a handy way to add inserts to a book. I created the insert on the left page of the altered book, complete with a mesh window with a view of the American flag on the previous page. Then I cut part of a page out of the altered book and stitched the insert onto the flap. I could have attached it with tape, but the stitches seemed to go well with the Victorian images.

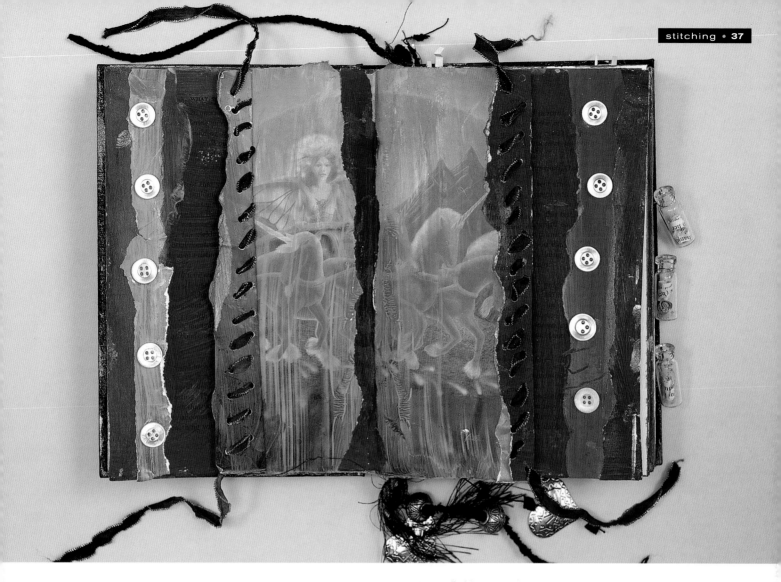

ABOVE: On either side of this spread I used just one strand of fiber, which transitions between colors picked up from the rest of the design. Although the folded pages really are just glued together, the stitches and buttons appear to be what holds them in place.

LEFT: I used the stitching on these pages strictly for decorative purposes. I wove strands of fiber in vertical rows and around the circular image in the middle. Notice that this image is slightly off center to the right. The two vertical rows of fiber on the left balance this effect. To cover up the stitching on the backs of these pages, I simply glued them to the adjacent pages.

Cutting Doors

Doors are interactive, drawing the observer into the page. I have to open every door I see in an altered book because I want to know what's behind it. Knowing this, I try to make what is behind my doors as interesting as the doors themselves.

✂ MATERIALS 3 pages of your book; collage image; craft knife with a new blade; cutting mat; flat paintbrush; ink pad; PVA glue; ruler; rubber stamp with a shape that can serve as a door

1 PLACE THE DOORS • Paint the back of page 1, all of page 2, and the front of page 3. You can use any stamp that has a frame or borders that will form the frame of your door. Stamp the front of page 2 wherever you want the door to appear.

2 CUT THE OPENING • Place a cutting mat between pages 2 and 3 and align a ruler vertically in the center of the door frame. Hold the ruler in place and use a craft knife to cut a line down the center of the shape to create double doors.

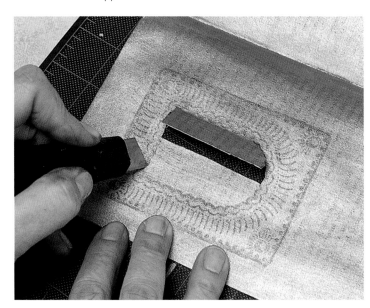

3 CUT ALONG THE TOP AND BOTTOM • Cut along the top and bottom of each door so it is attached to the page only on one side. Clean up rough edges if necessary. Fold the doors open and crease them along the edges. This fold will be just irresistible to anyone looking through your book.

TIP! When placing an image behind the door, use one that is bigger than the door to make sure you fill the frame. As you become more experienced, you can plan ahead to use an image that fits not only the door, but also the design for the page behind the door.

4 GIVE THE VIEWERS A VIEW • Place an image on the front of page 3 behind the door. Center it as you wish, checking to see how it looks through the door. Apply glue to the back of the image with a flat brush and glue it onto page 3. Then glue pages 2 and 3 together. When the door opens, you'll see the image through it.

Variations

RIGHT: This door is more complex than most, so I decorated the rest of the page with simple glazing and a few rubber stamps. This page interestingly lets you see one character clearly while the other is visible but blocked by the door. It makes the viewer really want to open the door to get a clear view of the woman behind it.

BELOW: Just because many buildings have only one door doesn't mean that you have to limit yourself that way! I built eight doors here, and the numbers make viewers want to open them even more. I placed old-fashioned family photos behind my doors.

ABOVE: Both the mesh and feathers have a brown metallic color, so they go together well. I also placed a slightly tarnished gold embellishment on each page, one near the top of the left page and one near the bottom of the right page. Hints of gold paint over the purple background bring out the gold in the embellishments and the metallic feel of the mesh and feathers.

LEFT: This door is on an insert instead of the actual book page. The clock is made of simple materials: wide-ruled paper, pencil and black construction paper. Even though the door isn't open, you can see the black pendulums through the old paper. The clock indicates the passage of time, which goes well with the old pictures and the antique feel of the collage paper.

Cutting Windows

Like doors, windows draw the observer into the page. While a door gives a viewer an exclusive view of the image behind it, a window's view is obvious immediately, and you can see through a window from both directions. You can create a window without thought to what is behind it, or you can place it to let viewers see an interesting part of the following page's design.

✂ MATERIALS 4 pages of your book; acetate; bone folder; collage images; craft knife; cutting mat; flat paintbrush; pencil; PVA glue; ruler

1 PLACE THE WINDOW • Paint the four pages. On the front of page 2, outline the window you want to make. It can be square, rectangular, vertical, horizontal, abstract—any shape you want.

2 CUT THE WINDOW • Place a cutting mat behind both pages 2 and 3. Use a craft knife to cut along the pencil lines, cutting through both pages. If you want to cut perfectly straight lines, place a ruler next to the line to guide the knife.

3 OPEN THE WINDOW • Remove the sections of the pages you cut out. Clean up the edges with a craft knife if necessary.

TIP! For a simpler way to cut a window, use a large hole punch. For a more complex technique, cut little squares instead of one big one to form frames for panes of glass.

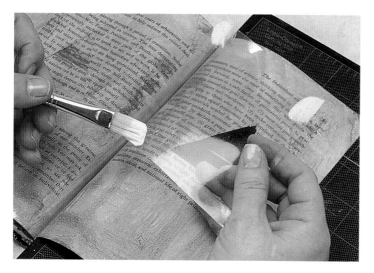

4 APPLY GLUE TO THE ACETATE • Cut a piece of acetate larger than the openings you cut out. It doesn't have to be the same shape as long as it covers the opening. Apply glue to each corner of the acetate with a brush.

5 INSERT THE "GLASS" • Place the acetate over the opening on the front of page 3. Burnish, or smooth, the corners with your hands to make sure the acetate is in place. You don't have to wait for the glue to dry to move on.

6 GLUE THE PAGES • Apply PVA glue to the back of page 2 with a brush. You don't have to get close to the window opening. You just need enough glue to adhere the pages together.

7 ADHERE THE PAGES • Close page 2 over page 3 and burnish them together with a bone folder.

8 CREATE A "VIEW" • Use PVA glue and a brush to glue an image onto the back of page 1 and another to the front of page 4 so you can see an image through either side of the window.

9 LOOK BOTH WAYS • Notice how the window frames each image. Each spread has one image with soft, textured edges and one image within a frame. You can incorporate each image into its own page design without affecting how it will look through this frame.

Variations

RIGHT: A mesh screen forms the "glass" for this window, which looks out at a solemn woman. The black-and-white image behind the window, as it contrasts with the bright color of the rest of the page, adds to her seriousness. I liked the visual format of the book's table of contents and let it show through the color.

BELOW: Windows don't have to be rectangular and neat. The shape of a window, whether regular or irregular, can add to your interpretation of the image behind it.

ABOVE: Here, I cut not just a frame but also window panes. The window looks partially open without panes at the bottom, but I like how the panes frame the girl's face at the top. The purple contrasts nicely with the black-and-white image and the muted colors of the other image, all coming together to create an inviting page.

LEFT: The two faces you see through this window are used in a similar way on the page behind it. Notice that the word "believe" is stamped between the two windows. The same word is spelled out with tags that hang off the edge of the next page. If you're working on a theme, remember that you don't have to limit that theme just to the page you're working on.

TIP! You can save the parts of the pages you cut out for collaging on other pages in your book. The shapes make interesting additions to a collage, especially if you painted the page before you cut the window out. To give the page more of a window feel, you can add curtains or other window treatments. You can use a variety of materials for your window. Mesh or any transparent material will work.

Adding Tags

Turning small tags of all sizes and shapes into small works of art has become very popular in the past few years. I must admit that I like tags and feel that they make a great addition to any altered book. I'm always looking for ways to add interest to my altered books, and tags do the trick. This technique will show you how to make a "page" of tags. You can look at all three tags at once or turn them separately.

✂ MATERIALS 5 pages of your book; double-stick tape; ink pad; scissors; scrap piece of paper; rubber stamps; three tags

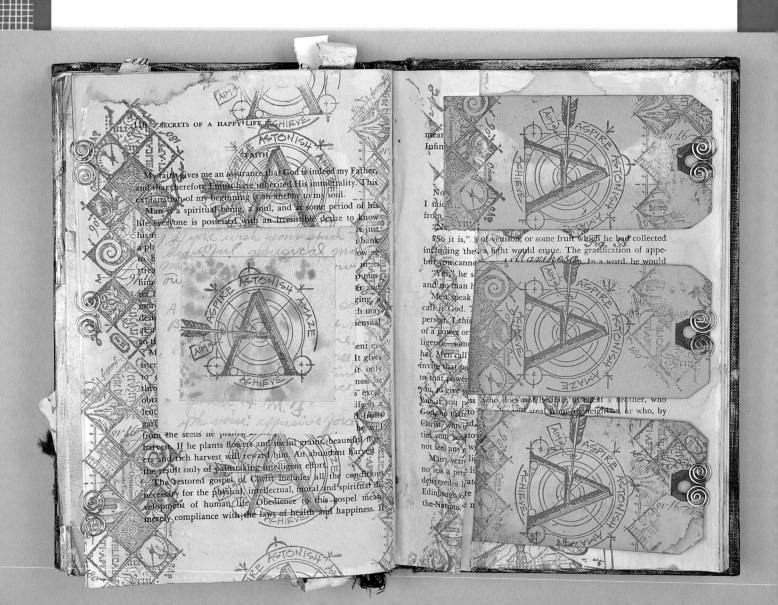

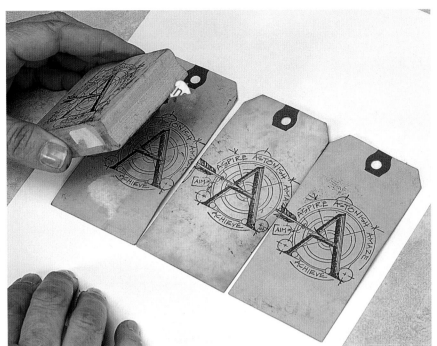

1 DECORATE THE TAGS •
Choose three tags of the same size and
rubber stamp both sides. Sometimes
you'll glue tags to a page or stick them
in a pocket, but for this technique you'll
be able to see both sides of each tag as
you flip through the book.

TIP! I dye almost
all of my tags by soak-
ing them in strong tea before I work
on them. I like the way this changes
the look and texture of a plain tag.

2 ADD ANOTHER LAYER OF STAMPS •
I like to add another dimension to my tags with more
stamps. You get a feeling that you're not limited by
edges or boundaries when the stamps overlap the
edges of the tags.

3 REMOVE A FEW PAGES • Holding pages 2, 3 and 4
together, start to cut them off about 3 inches (8 centimeters) from
the spine.

4 CREATE FLAPS • Finish removing the pages. You now have three flaps of paper, one for each tag.

5 ATTACH A TAG TO EACH FLAP • Apply double-stick tape (you could also use glue) to the back of one of the tags and attach it to the front of the first flap, close to the top of the book. Attach another tag to the second flap, centering between the top and bottom edges of the book.

6 ADD THE LAST TAG • Apply the last tag to the last flap, near the bottom. When the book is open to the first tag, the three tags seem to form one page, but a viewer also can turn the tags separately, like getting more for their money. Decorate the two full pages on either side of the flaps to complete the design.

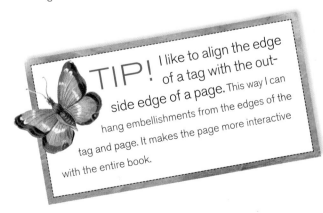

TIP! I like to align the edge of a tag with the outside edge of a page. This way I can hang embellishments from the edges of the tag and page. It makes the page more interactive with the entire book.

Variations

LEFT: I love to rubber stamp on tags. The size and shape of tags add the three-dimensional feel that I love. With that taken care of, I can play on the two-dimensional surface of the individual tags with my stamps. I stamped butterflies all over this page: on the background, as a large central image on the left and in a scattered pattern on the tags.

BELOW: Tags can be all different sizes, and they don't have to hang off pages. Here I glued a rubber stamped tag over a piece of black cardstock that acts as a border. I used similar stamps to decorate the paper dolls and then glued their arms and legs into interesting poses. The fibers tied around their legs imitate the tags hanging off other pages in the book.

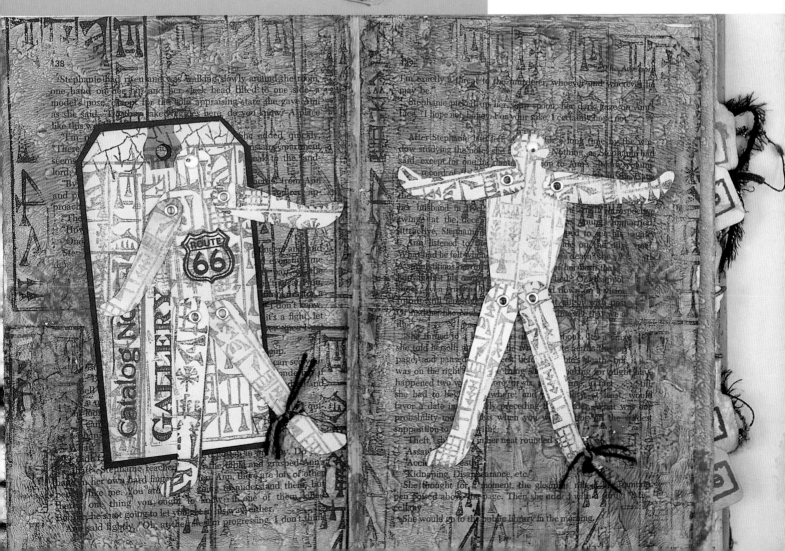

Folding Pages

Folding pages is an easy and effective way to add another dimension to your book. You can tape folded pages to other pages or leave them free to function as separate, interestingly-shaped pages. You can form pockets to hold embellishments, a wonderful way to make the page interactive for your viewers.

✂ **MATERIALS** 4 pages of your book; double-stick tape; 8 medium-sized tags; ink pads; rubber stamp

1 FOLD THE CORNERS IN • Paint the four pages. Turn to the back of page 3 and the front of page 4. Fold the bottom left corner of page 3 at an angle toward the center of the book. Crease the fold when the corner is halfway up the height of the page. The corner probably won't reach the spine. Fold the top corner of the page down toward the center of the spine the same way. The two corners should meet.

2 REPEAT THE FOLDS ON THE OTHER PAGE • Turn to the back of page 1 and the front of page 2. Fold the corners of page 2 toward the spine to match the folds you made in step 1. Crease these folds.

3 LOOK AT YOUR DESIGN • Turn to the back of page 2 and the front of page 3. You now have symmetrical folds. When taped down, these folded pages will form pockets that can hold anything you want to put there.

4 ATTACH TAPE • Turn again to the back of page 3, which is folded down. Run double-stick tape across the top, middle and bottom of the page from the spine to the other edge. Remove the adhesive backing.

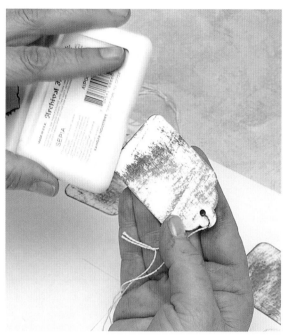

5 FORM POCKETS • Press page 3 down to page 4, applying pressure along the taped areas to adhere the pages. You now have two pockets between pages 3 and 4. Tape pages 1 and 2 together the same way.

6 INK THE TAGS • Apply ink to your tags by pressing the ink pad onto the tags (you don't always have to use rubber stamps to apply ink!). This just adds some interesting texture.

7 STAMP THE TAGS • Using the same or different colored ink, rubber stamp your tags. The defined pattern from a stamp contrasts nicely with the texture from the direct-to-paper technique you used in step 6. Decorate the tags however else you'd like.

8 INSERT THE TAGS INTO THE POCKETS • Place two tags in each pocket. You can tape or glue them into place or leave them loose for viewers to play with.

TIP! Experiment folding your pages in different ways. You might surprise yourself and come up with a new and unique design.

Variations

LEFT: Diagonal folds are fun to play with. There actually are four pieces of brown paper here, but each pair forms a rectangle and together look like one piece of paper. The papers closest to the spine are folded into the diagonally folded book pages. The pieces of brown paper closest to the edges of the book are inserted into pockets formed by the folded pages.

BELOW: Here I folded just one page of the spread. I imitated the triangular point by layering diamond-shaped papers and blocks of color. These pointed shapes contrast the circular shape on the left side. Notice that the beads hanging off the folded page's point add a bit of dimension to the page and to the book. Notice that you can see a bit of the next page as well. Good altered pages always make you a little curious about what's coming next.

Adding Inserts

Adding inserts is a great way to showcase that card someone special sent you or that postcard you just couldn't pass up. It's better than sticking them in a shoebox! You also can add pages from another book or introduce an entirely different feel with delicate papers that contrast the coarse feeling of the original book pages. Inserts are most interesting when they're noticeably different in size or shape from the original pages.

✂ MATERIALS 3 pages of your book; ⅛-inch (3mm) hole punch; card or other insert; cutting mat; dental floss threader; fiber; pencil; scissors

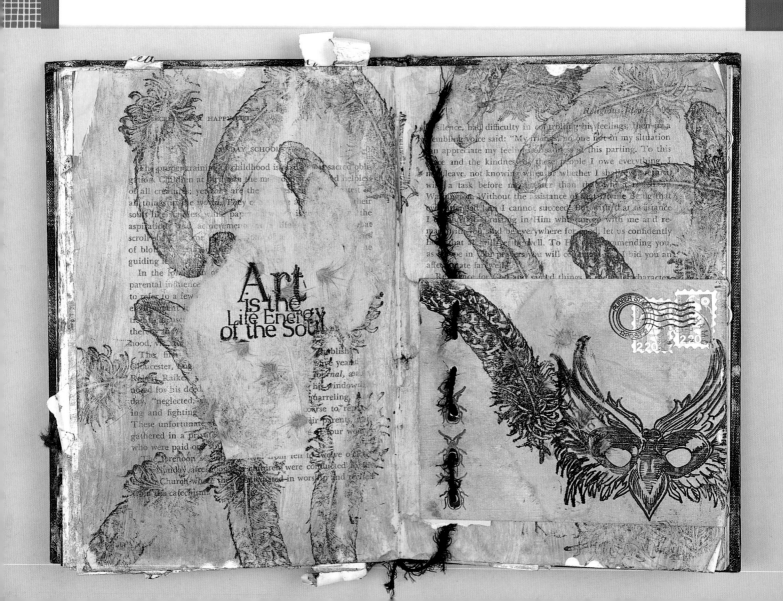

1 PUNCH THE CARD • Paint the back of page 1, all of page 2 and the front of page 3, and decorate an insert any way you'd like. Punch holes along the left side of the insert with your hole punch. If you're using a Japanese screw punch, remember to use a cutting mat now and in step 3.

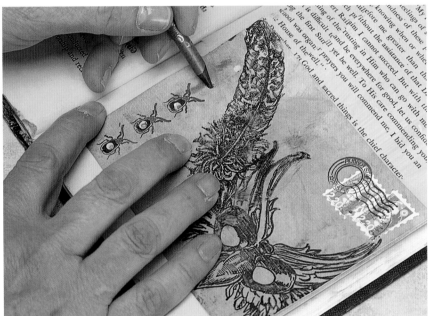

2 MARK THE HOLES • Cut out page 2, leaving a flap about 2 inches (5 centimeters) wide in the spine. Place the card over the flap where you want to attach it. Use a pencil to mark the page through the holes you punched in the card.

3 PUNCH THE PAGE • Remove the card and punch holes in the flap according to these marks.

TIP! If you punch an even number of holes, the end of the fiber will come out the same side of the page as you started. If you punch an uneven number of holes, the fiber will finish on the opposite side.

4 ATTACH THE CARD • Put the card back over the flap, lining up the holes in the flap and in the card. Using a dental floss threader, weave a piece of fiber through the holes to connect the card to the page flap.

5 SECURE THE INSERT • Tie knots in the fiber at the top and bottom of the card to hold the fiber and insert in place. You can cut the fiber off immediately above the knot or leave a tail to add interest.

6 REMOVE THE FLAP • Both above and below the insert, tear the flap from the edge to the spine and remove those pieces of the flap from the book. This conceals the way the insert is attached. Decorate the full pages on either side of the insert to complete the design. The insert functions as its own page and also complements the pages visible on either side.

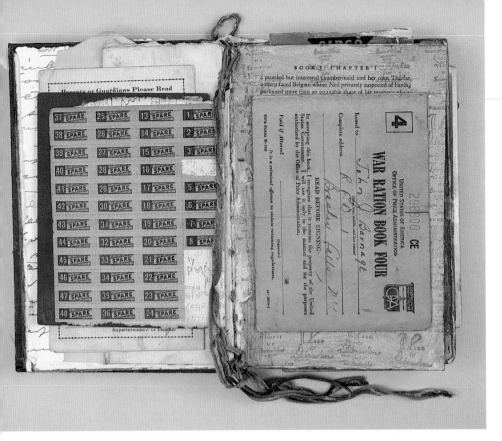

Variations

LEFT: These rationing coupons are the last of several inserts I added in one spot in the book. Old pictures, correspondence and even a report card from 1926 all are attached to the fibers you see along the spine. The fibers are threaded through other pages in front of and behind the inserts to attach them to the book itself.

BELOW: The mesh insert on the left matches the pieces of mesh I've wrapped around the edge of the page on the right. First I painted the spread purple and used a piece of chicken wire and paint to imprint a larger pattern on the spread. Then I ripped off part of the left page to create a flap with a ragged edge and attached the mesh to the flap.

· chapter · · · · · three · · ·

Intermediate Techniques

The techniques in this chapter build on the skills you gathered in Chapter 2. Not only will you learn specific techniques, but you'll start to come up with your own ideas for ways to implement all those fun looks you're imagining. But don't be nervous: These techniques aren't difficult either.

The painting techniques in this chapter will add sophistication to your pages. Transparent glazes allow the book's text to show through. Layering a few glazes adds an artsy effect. Texturing makes the difference between a flat page and a page with depth.

Cutting shadowboxes and niches provide impact. Let's face it: If you want to change a two-dimensional surface, isn't the best way to make it three-dimensional? Cut or collage your altered book cover to really draw your viewers into your book. Make your book's first impression a good one.

Cutting Shadowboxes

You can use a shadowbox to hold large embellishments or objects that would not otherwise fit into an altered book. Create a shadowbox by making a deep cut into a block of pages. This typically uses most of the pages in a book. Or create a niche by cutting a shallower hole.

✂ **MATERIALS** large group of pages in your book; bulldog clips; collage papers; craft knife and extra blade; cutting mat; flat paintbrushes; gel medium; pencil; ruler; three-dimensional embellishments; violet gold acrylic paint

1 BIND THE PAGES • It's best to use the front or back cover of the book as the bottom of your box to provide the best support, so gather a group of pages that begins or ends with a page next to a cover. The thickness of this group determines the depth of your box. Use a flat brush to apply gel medium to the side, top and bottom edges of this group of pages.

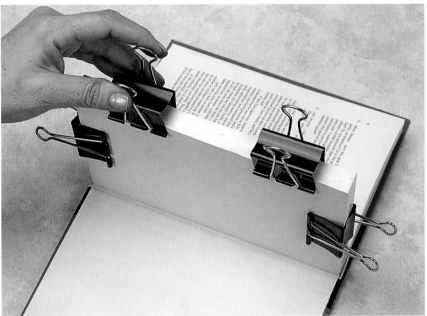

2 LET THE PAGES DRY • Hold the pages closed with bulldog clips while the adhesive dries, approximately twenty to thirty minutes.

TIP! Before you start cutting, make sure you have a new blade in your craft knife. The sharper the blade, the easier it is to cut through the block. You may even want to change blades again halfway through.

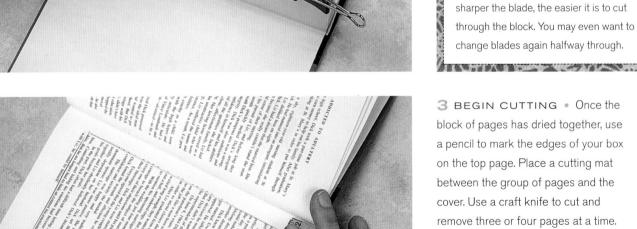

3 BEGIN CUTTING • Once the block of pages has dried together, use a pencil to mark the edges of your box on the top page. Place a cutting mat between the group of pages and the cover. Use a craft knife to cut and remove three or four pages at a time. Lay a ruler along the pencil line as a guide to help you cut a straight line.

4 CUT OUT THE REMAINING PAGES • Continue cutting and removing small groups of paper until you've cut through the entire block of pages.

5 APPLY GLUE TO THE BLOCK OF PAGES • Open the book to the back cover. This book happened to come with red endsheets. Apply gel medium to the back of the block of pages with a flat brush.

6 GLUE IT TO THE COVER • Glue the pages to the cover with gel medium. Turn the book over and press firmly along the edges of the cover to make sure it adheres to the pages.

TIP! Don't worry about cutting clean edges while you're hollowing out your box. You can clean up the entire edge once you've cut through all of the pages.

7 APPLY SOME COLOR • Apply paint to the top of the block of pages and the facing page with another flat brush.

8 COVER THE INSIDE OF THE BOX • Using gel medium, glue one of the page scraps that you removed in steps 3 and 4 to cover the bottom of the shadowbox. You also could cover the inside of the box with more paint.

9 ADD SOME COLLAGE MATERIALS • Add collage materials as you wish, using gel medium and a flat brush.

10 ADD EMBELLISHMENTS • Shadowboxes are great for holding three-dimensional embellishments. Decorate the rest of the page any way you'd like.

Variations

RIGHT: Two similar images make up this spread, but one lies in a shallow niche that allows just enough room to glue a fairly flat three-dimensional embellishment over it. The musical instrument adds a nice touch. It looks like something an angel would play, doesn't it?

BELOW: I used all of the pages in this book to make this shadowbox. Hanging collage paper over the edges of the opening creates shadows that make the shadowbox effect even more obvious. I added three-dimensional embellishments on the left page so both sides of the spread complement each other. Normally, the embellishments on the left side would keep the book from closing, but here they work because they fall within the perimeters of the box.

ABOVE: Altered books are a wonderful place to put souvenirs and other objects that just don't seem to belong anywhere else. I cut a small niche into this book to store starfish I picked up near my new home on the beach. Seashells, seaweed and even sand finish out this page's coastal theme.

LEFT: This niche holds nothing but an image, though it's surrounded by three-dimensional embellishments. I removed a good number of pages from the middle of this spread to make room for them so the book would close. Notice that the left side is flat, though a feeling of depth is suggested by layered papers and glazes.

TIP! Your box doesn't have to be square, and it doesn't have to be centered. Make it any shape or size you like, and place it anywhere on the page.

Glazing

Glazes are great for altered books, especially. Because glazes are translucent, they let text and images from the book or your collages show through. Layering glazes gives your pages a more sophisticated look. I like to use three of four layers of glaze on a page, sometimes adding collage images and papers between them. I alternate layers of warm colors (red, orange and yellow) and cool colors (blue, violet and green). Otherwise the colors turn muddy.

MATERIALS 2 pages of your book; collage images; collage papers; flat paintbrush; bright yellow, purple, sea foam green, violet earth and yellow ochre glazes; paper towel; PVA glue

1 ADD THE FIRST (WARM) LAYER • Apply a layer of yellow ochre glaze over both pages with a flat brush. When the paint is dry, add any collage images, text and papers you wish with a flat brush and PVA glue. Let this layer dry.

2 ADD THE SECOND (COOL) LAYER • Add a coat of sea foam green glaze, covering the entire page, including the collage items. Let the glaze dry.

3 ADD THE THIRD (WARM) LAYER • Paint violet earth glaze over the entire page, allowing a bit of the previous layer to show through.

TIP! Make sure you let each layer dry before applying the next one. Otherwise the colors will mix together and become muddy.

4 EVALUATE THE BIG PICTURE • You can add more collage images at any point in the glazing process. I felt that this composition needed another image, so I just glued it right over the previous layers.

5 ADD THE FOURTH (COOL) LAYER • Apply a coat of purple glaze. I painted a thicker coat over the new image to make it "sink" back into the page.

6 LIFT PAINT • I wanted the image of the butterfly and the words to stick out, so, before the paint dried, I used a paper towel to dab and lift some of the purple glaze from these areas.

7 ADD THE FINAL (WARM) LAYER • Keeping with the practice of alternating warm and cool colors, apply a final layer of bright yellow glaze. The yellow lightens the entire piece.

TIP! You can visually push an image back or pull it out by varying the amount of glaze you apply over it. Applying a thicker coat over an image than over the rest of the page will blend it in. Applying less glaze will help the image stand out a bit. You also can lift or wipe glaze off an image that you want to show more.

TIP! Layering glazes and images and letting previous colors show through gives your page an interactive feel. Don't be afraid to experiment with the glazes. Try adding one thick layer and the next one thinner. Or add two thick layers or thin layers. I also like to vary the thickness of the glaze within one layer. You can even cover a collage element that didn't work out with a thick layer of glaze.

Variations

LEFT: There actually are two images on this spread. The one on the right has much less glaze over it, so it stands out as the main image. In fact, it almost keeps you from seeing the image on the left. Collage paper surrounds and even overlaps the bottom of the main image, but the glaze brings the collage paper and the image together, creating a seamless look. Glazes can do so much to bring elements together or help them stand out.

BELOW: These glazes give an iridescent shimmer to the pages and the white washers. The gradations between the colors of glazes also follow the vertical flow of the columns of washers. Notice that the columns use smaller washers and more of them as you move from right to left.

Adding Texture

Using paint or ink to add texture to a page adds a subtle effect that can really bring a page together. Any tool or material you can use to move paint around or apply it in an interesting pattern will work. I like to stipple paint to create a background or to add a pattern over a design to bring it together. To stipple, hold a stipple brush vertically and dab it onto the surface. I like to use ink when stippling because it dries so much faster than paint. Look at pages 76 and 77 to see other ways to add texture to your pages.

✂ MATERIALS 2 pages of your book; cardstock or paper; dark brown, golden brown and ochre ink pads; rubber stamps; three stipple brushes

1 APPLY THE FIRST LAYER OF TEXTURE •
Pounce the stipple brush up and down on an ochre ink
pad until you have enough ink on the brush. Practice
stippling in your practice book. Once you know how
much ink to put on your brush to get an even applica-
tion on your page, you can move onto your real altered
page. Holding the brush vertically, repeat the pouncing
motion on the page. Continue stippling until you have a
nice coat of ink on the page.

2 APPLY A SECOND LAYER • Using golden brown ink, stipple
over the ochre ink. Let some of the first layer show through. Ink dries
so quickly that you don't really have to worry about letting the ink from
step 1 dry.

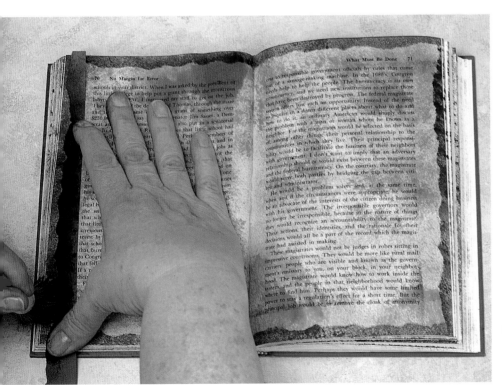

3 CREATE A BORDER • Tear a
strip of cardstock or paper and lay it on
the page, leaving a gap at the edge for
the border. Let the uneven side of the
torn paper face outward. This paper will
mask the page so you can create an
interesting border. Hold the paper in
place as you stipple along the edge of
the page with dark brown ink.

TIP! To create
a border
that is lighter instead
of darker than the rest of
the page, mask the edge of the
page and stipple the rest of the page
inside of the mask.

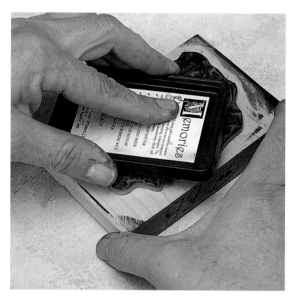

4 TEST SOME COLOR SCHEMES • To determine which ink you'd like to use for your rubber stamping, stamp different colors of ink on the next page of your book or onto scrap paper. Hold this test page next to the one you're altering to see how they go together.

5 APPLY INK TO THE STAMP • I decided to carry the color of the border over to the rubber stamping. Apply the same dark brown ink to a rubber stamp. For larger stamps, it's sometimes easier and cleaner to rub the ink onto the stamp rather than rubbing the stamp over the ink.

6 BRING THE PAGE TOGETHER • The stippling technique provided a nice textured background. Now stamp your image onto the page to bring the composition and color scheme together.

Variations

LEFT: I used a rich green to complement the references to Ireland in the quote and the clovers on the right and bottom left. The copper/rust color complements this green. Stippling with both of these colors gave the page an interesting and grainy, vintage look.

BELOW: This entire spread is stippled with a few different colors. Notice that the stippling is more apparent in the lighter areas. Just a bit of stippling over the stained glass window and the lettering yields a grainy, photographed look. Heavier stippling over the background lends an abstract, artsy flair.

Other Texturing Techniques

Look at the supplies around your home and in stores in a new light to find materials for texturing. Be creative. Anything that will imprint, lift or move paint around can be used to texture your pages.

Sponging

Use sponges to apply a solid, textured color over the entire background, to add accent color over other layers or to create interesting shapes.

Inking
Use bottles of ink to paint loose, fun shapes on a page. You can even press ink-patterned pages together and then peel them apart to form a symmetrical shape on a spread. Remember that ink dries fairly quickly.

Faux Texturing
When pressed into wet paint, crinkled plastic wrap creates a nice faux texture.

Imprinting
Look for textured surfaces around your house that would make interesting imprints for a background or over images. Bubble wrap, mesh and even scraps of textured wallpaper leave fun marks in wet paint.

Collaging Covers

Collaging a cover is different from collaging an interior page. As you work on your collage, keep in mind that the cover is a three-dimensional surface. Viewers can see the front cover or back cover individually, or they can pick up the book and look at all the different sides as one. There are so many possibilities when working on multiple planes.

✂ MATERIALS front and back cover of your book; bone folder; collage images; collage papers; fine grain sandpaper; flat paintbrush; PVA glue; three-dimensional embellishments

1 PREPARE THE SURFACE • Lightly sand the surface of the book to remove grease and dirt left from fingerprints and handling. This gives the cover a more uniform look and makes it better suited for adhesives.

2 PREPARE THE IMAGES • You also can lightly sand any images that are glossy. It's not necessary; it just depends on the look you want.

3 COVER THE SPINE • Lay the paper you want to use on your work surface with the front side down. Lay the book on top of the paper and wrap the paper around the spine as if you were wrapping a present. Wrapping one piece of paper around both sides of the book helps the viewer understand the multiple dimensions of an altered book.

TIP! In addition to sanding the covers, you also can apply a coat of gesso before you add collage papers and images. Like primer, gesso helps paints and glue adhere to the surface.

4 DETERMINE THE WIDTH OF THE PAPER • Align the paper around the spine, and cut the excess off the sides. The paper can extend across either side as far as you want it to go.

5 TRIM THE TOP AND BOTTOM EDGES • Align the paper with the bottom of the book and cut the excess off the top.

6 DECIDE WHAT LOOK YOU WANT • Tearing the vertical edges of my collage paper made for a more interesting look. It matches the scruffy look I achieved by sanding the glossy image in step 2.

7 GLUE THE PAPER TO THE BOOK • Now that you've trimmed your collage paper, glue it to the book with PVA glue and a flat brush. If you apply glue to the back of the paper instead of to the book you're less likely to apply it to places where you don't need it.

8 GIVE THE PAPER A TIGHTER FIT • While the glue is still wet, use a bone folder to force the paper into the creases of the spine, which will give your book a nice finished look.

9 DECORATE THE REST OF THE COVER • Tear other collage papers and images and glue them into place. Overlapping elements add more interest, moving the viewer's eye from one item to another.

10 ADD COLOR • Add the main elements of your cover: a larger image and perhaps some three-dimensional embellishments. I call this cover "Vegas." I like that the black-and-white scheme contrasts with the bright color of the dice.

Variations

RIGHT: This book is completely finished. You can see how much the fibers I've used between pages and the embellishments I've hung from the edges of pages contribute to a book's overall feel. All I've done to the cover itself is to layer one piece of collage paper, one image and one piece of text along with an interesting strand of fiber.

BELOW: I glazed and imprinted this cover first and then applied a simple collage image and embellishments without layering. Alphabet tile collage paper is available, but I like the three-dimensional feel of actual Scrabble game tiles to add more dimension.

TIP! You can cut and glue images haphazardly, or you can arrange and plan your entire cover before gluing anything down. And don't forget to work on the back cover, too! Covers take more abuse than any other part of your book. Make them as sturdy as possible. Avoid using fragile paper and embellishments.

ABOVE: This entire book is made of nothing but glazes and washers. Some of the washers are covered with glazes, and some are glued over glazes.

LEFT: This cover uses just one image, which is complex enough to stand on its own. Sometimes, one image or even just one layer of paint or collage paper is all you need.

Cutting Covers

Cutting a hole into the cover of a book adds a lot of interest and introduces viewers to the three-dimensional quality of altered books. This is especially true when you place embellishments or images behind the hole.

✂ MATERIALS

front cover of your book; cutting mat; craft knife with a new blade; E6000 glue or gel medium; flat paintbrushes; found embellishments; green acrylic paint; pencil; PVA glue; ruler

1 MARK THE EDGES OF YOUR HOLE • Paint the cover with green or any other color you'd like. Use a pencil and ruler to mark the position of the hole.

2 CUT THE HOLE • Place a cutting mat inside the cover to protect the pages of the book. Cut through the cover with a craft knife, using the ruler as a guide to cut straight lines.

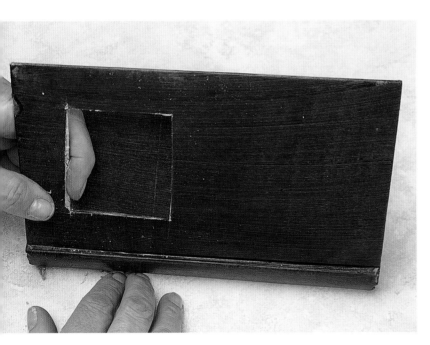

3 REMOVE THE BOARD • Push the cut piece through the front of the book to leave a clean edge on the outside of the front cover.

4 CLEAN UP THE EDGES • Use the craft knife to clean up the inside of the cover and any pieces left in the corners.

TIP! Be patient while cutting. It will take several cuts to get through. As usual, a new blade for the craft knife is invaluable.

5 PAINT THE INNER EDGES • Paint the edges of the area you cut out. Or you can wait to paint the entire cover and the edges of the hole until after you've cut it.

6 PLACE AN IMAGE BEHIND THE HOLE • Place an image on the first page of the book to show through the hole you've cut. Once you've positioned it as you'd like, glue the image down with PVA glue and a flat brush.

7 FRAME THE "PICTURE" • Using E6000 glue or gel medium, add embellishments to frame the image and window.

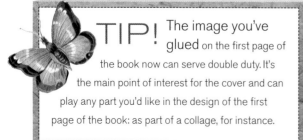

TIP! The image you've glued on the first page of the book now can serve double duty. It's the main point of interest for the cover and can play any part you'd like in the design of the first page of the book: as part of a collage, for instance.

8 ADD A FINISHING TOUCH • Add another embellishment to round out the cover.

Variations

LEFT: I made this altered book from a children's book with thick cardboard pages. I cut a big block out of the middle and collaged the frame of the hole with scraps of paper from another book. I added rust-colored paint in some places to pick up the warm color of the four corner embellishments, and I added just a bit of blue to the collage to pick up the blue embellishments covering the hole. The image behind the hole is part of a collage on the first interior page.

BELOW: Patriotic bathing beauties sit in the hole I cut in this cover. They add just enough raciness to the traditional patriotic theme to make it fun. The threads wrapped around the spine enhance this fun factor.

· · • chapter · · · four · · ·

Creative Techniques

Here you'll find great ideas and fantastic techniques that will take your art to the next level, inspiring you and transforming your book into a unique work of art.

Designing with words returns to the basic purpose of a book and thus is a powerful way to express your feelings. It also invites the observer into the page to stay awhile, reading and pondering the words you chose, appreciating them in conjunction with other design elements, such as rubber stamping and painting. Drawers give a book an interactive feel. Storing small objects in the drawers lets the observer not just look, but also play.

Hanging embellishments off the edges of the pages with eyelets adds volume to your book, communicating so much to an observer before he or she even picks up the book. Fibers and beads add that last punch of interesting texture or color to really bring your pages together. Transferring images and adding pop-ups are fun for the observer to see and for you to do. The techniques in this chapter are the ones that add the "Wow!" factor to your altered books.

Designing With Words

Designing with words is an easy way to make a verbal statement. A design with words draws the observer into your art. Sometimes a word or a phrase from the book you're altering will jump out and beg to be included in your design. You may use words scattered across a page to form a poem or express an idea. Or you can use entire quotes. Or if words from other pages go well with words from the page you're altering, cut them out and glue them here. Remember, the point is to alter the book. Don't limit yourself!

✂ MATERIALS 2 pages in your book; bright purple glaze; flat paintbrush; galaxy gold ink pad; Post-It Labeling and Cover-up Tape; PVA glue; rubber stamp

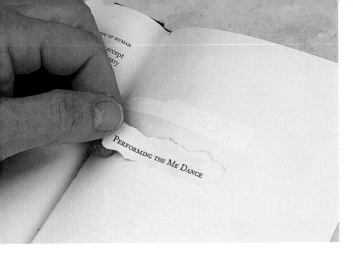

1 MASK THE WORDS • You'll be masking words or phrases to protect them from layers of paint, glaze, collage elements or rubber stamping you're going to apply. Choose the words you want to emphasize and cover them with Post-It tape. I liked a phrase that already appeared on this page and found another phrase elsewhere in the book that complemented it. I glued this second phrase onto the page with a flat brush and PVA glue, then masked both phrases.

2 APPLY SOME COLOR • Glaze bright purple over the entire page, including the tape with a flat brush. Let the paint air dry.

3 DECORATE THE PAGE • Before removing the mask, add any other decorations that you don't want to affect the highlighted words, such as a rubber stamp. I stamped with galaxy gold ink, which complements the purple glaze without competing with the words for attention.

4 REMOVE THE MASK • Carefully peel the tape off the page to reveal the words you preserved. Notice how much they stand out. As you lift the tape, you might notice that some paint seeped under. Not to worry, though: The ragged effect is interesting. Also, for a different look, you could glue down a phrase after applying color.

TIP! Although hair dryers and heat guns are good ways to speed up the drying process for paints and glazes, don't use them on a page with masked areas. The intense heat can permanently adhere the tape to the page. When you try to remove the mask, your carefully preserved words will come up with it.

Variations

RIGHT: You can see the text of this book page through the metallic purple glaze, but the words I masked really stand out. They have meaning separately, but put together they also can reflect your mood or paint a "portrait" of yourself or someone you're thinking of.

BELOW: You can add your own words to a page to complement elements that you've added. This man was mysterious to me; I didn't know quite what to make of him. You can see the words that came to mind as I looked at him.

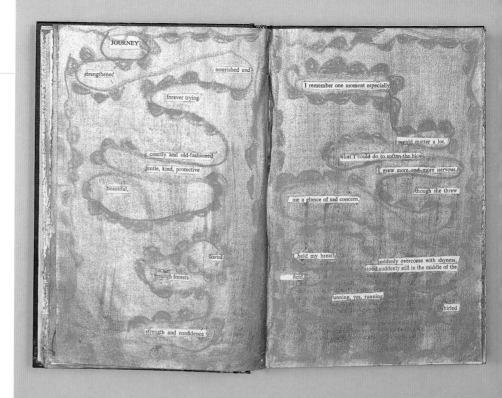

ABOVE: A particular phrase that I found in an advertisement really stuck out to me. I used it in a collage that also included a musical composition. This design indicates that you can communicate not just with words or visuals but also with sounds. The view of overlapping elements through the window also adds depth to the page.

LEFT: One large phrase stuck out to me on this page, so I let it show through the glaze. You can't see any other words from the original page. I like the resulting impact this makes.

Adding Drawers

I love the idea of drawers in a book. I think they add a new dimension and a fun way to include embellishments. I've always used matchboxes to hold tiny handmade books or pocket shrines. When I started doing altered books, the idea of putting matchboxes in a book rather than putting books in matchboxes appealed to me. This is a fun technique that is well worth the work it takes to create it.

MATERIALS large group of pages in your book; antique gold spray paint; bulldog clips; craft knife and three fresh blades; cutting mat; E6000 glue; flat paintbrush; pencil; PVA glue; 3 beads for drawer handles; 3 matchboxes; toothpick

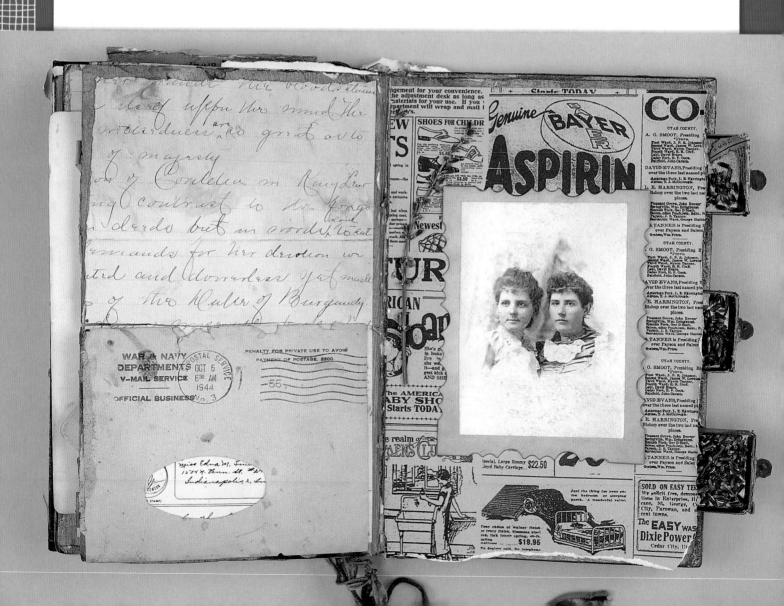

1 PAINT THE MATCHBOXES •
Remove the drawers from the matchbox
sleeves and spray paint them with gold
paint. Use a thin layer of paint, just enough
to cover them so the box still will slide in
and out of the sleeves. Let the paint dry.

2 GATHER PAGES • Hold the
short side of a matchbox next to a group
of pages. Gather a block of pages starting at the back of the book, and add
more until the thickness of the block
equals the thickness of the matchbox.

3 BIND THE PAGES • Apply PVA
glue to the edges of the block of pages
with a flat brush.

5 TRACE THE SHAPES OF THE MATCHBOXES • Place a matchbox on top of the block of pages, aligned with the edge of the page, and trace the shape with a pencil. Do this for each of the other two drawers. Remember to space them out.

4 LET THE GLUE DRY • Hold the pages together with bulldog clips until the adhesive dries.

6 BEGIN CUTTING • Place a cutting mat between the block of pages and the back cover of the book. Cut along the pencil lines, removing a few pages at a time. Don't worry about the cuts being super neat; they won't be visible on the finished product.

TIP! Even if I'm cutting a thick batch of pages, I always put my cutting mat in place first. It's so easy to forget about it as you get close to the bottom, and you don't want to cut the cover.

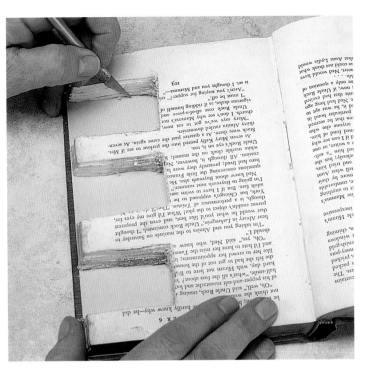

7 MAKE SURE THE MATCHBOX FITS • As you cut and remove small groups of pages, occasionally drop the matchbox into the hole to check that it fits. People seem to have a tendency to cut a narrower and narrower hole the deeper they cut.

8 FINISH CUTTING • Continue cutting until you've reached the cutting mat through all three holes. Clean up the corners and edges of each hole until the matchbox fits. It should fit snugly. Remember, the cuts don't have to be perfect.

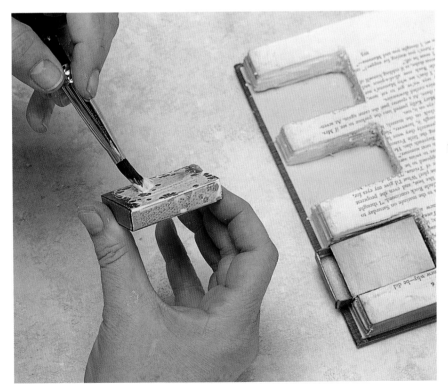

TIP! Make sure you have extra craft knife blades. This technique involves a lot of cutting. I suggest starting with a fresh blade and replacing it for each hole. It will make the whole process so much easier.

9 APPLY GLUE TO THE SLEEVES • Apply PVA glue to the bottoms and sides of the sleeves with a flat brush. Make sure you don't get glue on the drawers of the matchboxes or they might not open easily.

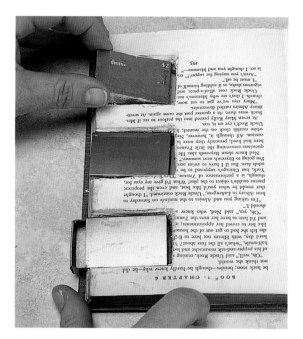

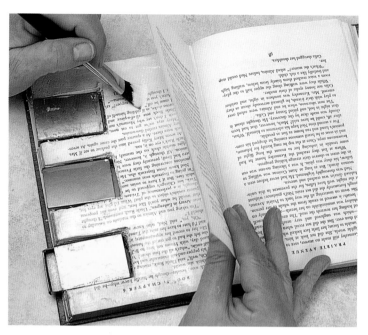

10 INSERT THE MATCHBOXES • Place each matchbox into an opening and press down to make sure it's secure in its new home.

11 COVER THE MATCHBOXES • Apply PVA glue to the tops of the page and boxes with a flat brush. Cover with the preceding page and press down to adhere them.

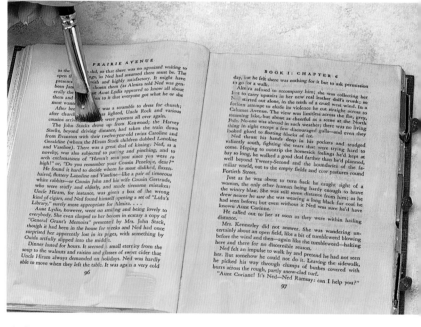

12 INSTALL THE HANDLES • Use a toothpick to apply just a little bit of E6000 glue to the beads you've chosen to serve as handles for your drawers. Press a bead to each drawer and hold firmly until it sticks. Let it dry for at least 30 minutes and test it to make sure it adhered well.

13 DECORATE THE TOP PAGES • Paint and decorate the top of your "dresser" with any of the other techniques in this book or a brilliant idea of your own.

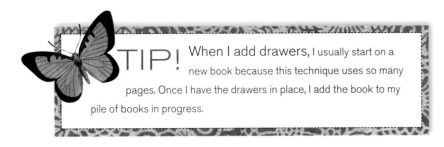

Variations

LEFT: You can put anything you want into these little drawers. Just place them in the drawer and let them jiggle around, or, as I did here, glue them down. I chose to glue these word beads in place because I like the flow of the words as I've organized them.

BELOW: Here I made one larger drawer out of a metal tin. It's sturdy enough that it didn't need a handle for the drawer. The drawer is filled with little Valentine's Day card envelopes. I let the brown paper from the page carry over to the bottom of the drawer. Some of the hearts are made of collage paper, some painted on. Behind the two layered hearts on the left page is another envelope with a tag and Valentine's Day greeting inside. Don't be afraid to combine techniques on one page.

little
girl
shine

you
run
wild

imagine
sing
dance

Hanging Embellishments

Hanging embellishments and papers from the edges of your book will give your viewers something interesting to look at even when it's closed. You can substitute any embellishment for the bottles I used here. The technique isn't hard; it just seems to use a lot of different pieces and materials. And the technique differs for every embellishment you want to hang. Just use your imagination to come up with creative ways to attach the embellishment.

✂ MATERIALS 2 pages in your book; cutting mat; eyelets; eyelet finisher (optional); eyelet setter; flat paintbrush; craft hammer; hole punch; needlenose pliers; pencil; PVA glue; small bottles; wire (20 to 24 gauge)

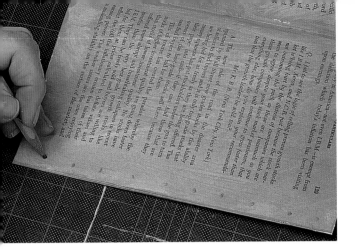

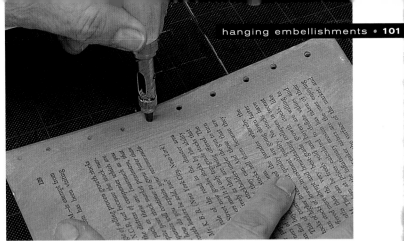

1 PLACE THE EYELETS • Paint the two pages any color you'd like. Decide where you want to place your eyelets and mark these spots with a pencil. Place them fairly close to the edge of the page since you'll be hanging embellishments off the edge.

2 PUNCH THE HOLES • Punch holes through your pencil marks using a hole punch. If you're using a Japanese screw punch instead, place a cutting mat behind the page first.

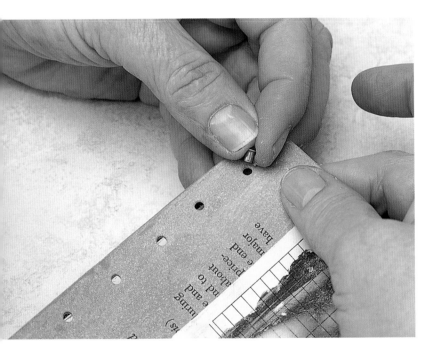

3 INSERT AN EYELET • Place an eyelet through one of the holes from the front through the back.

4 POSITION THE EYELET SETTER • Holding the eyelet in place, turn the page over and place a cutting mat under it. You should be looking at the back of the page and the back of the eyelet. Position the eyelet setter over the back of the eyelet.

6 FINISH IT OFF • Sometimes you'll need to finish setting the eyelet with an eyelet finisher and hammer or by lightly tapping the hammer directly on the back of the eyelet to remove any rough edges.

5 ATTACH THE EYELET • Pound the top of the eyelet setter with a hammer until the back of the eyelet is flat.

7 MAKE SCROLLS OF PAPER •
Repeat steps 3 through 6 to attach eyelets to each hole. Then rip a page out of your book or find any other piece of paper that has text on it. Cut the paper into strips and roll them into tight scrolls that will fit through the necks of the bottles. Slip the scrolls into the small bottles, pushing them through with a pencil if necessary.

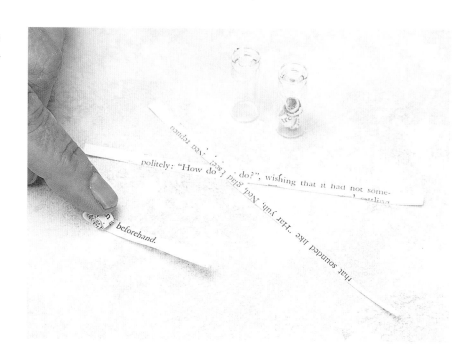

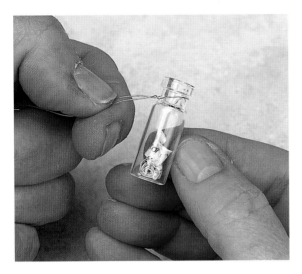

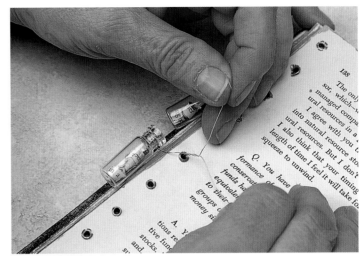

8 ATTACH THE BOTTLES TO THE WIRE • Cut a piece of wire 5 to 6 inches (13 to 15 centimeters) long. Wrap the center of the wire around the neck of one of the bottles and twist the wire together next to the neck of the bottle to lock it in place.

9 ATTACH THE WIRE TO THE EYELETS • Thread one end of the wire through the front of an eyelet. Pull it all the way through until the twisted wire lies at the end of the page. Wrap the other half of the wire around the edge of the page. Twist the wires together next to the back of the eyelet.

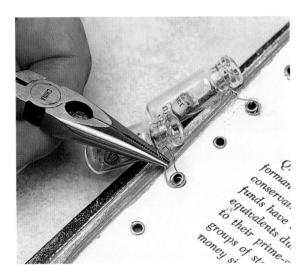

10 SECURE THE WIRE • Wrap the ends of the wire around the back of the eyelet with needlenose pliers to secure both the eyelet and the wire to the page.

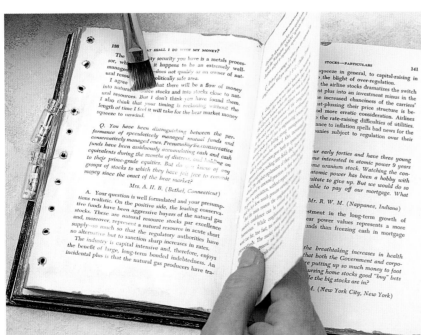

11 COVER UP YOUR MESS • Repeat steps 8 through 10 to attach a bottle to each eyelet. Apply glue to the back of the page with a flat brush and glue the following page to it, just like sweeping dust under a rug!

Variations

RIGHT: I let the text have impact on the left and the visuals have impact on the right. The red buttons seem to adhere pieces of paper that hang off the edge to the book page. These actually are scraps ripped from the margins of pages I'd ripped out of the book. Notice that the black, scribbly writing carries all the way across the spread to bring the design together.

BELOW: I love the feel of feathers. Hanging things off the edges of altered book pages gives observers not only something interesting to look at but also something that appeals to the sense of touch. I ripped about an inch from the left edge of the left page and then attached the feathers to bring the page back to its original width.

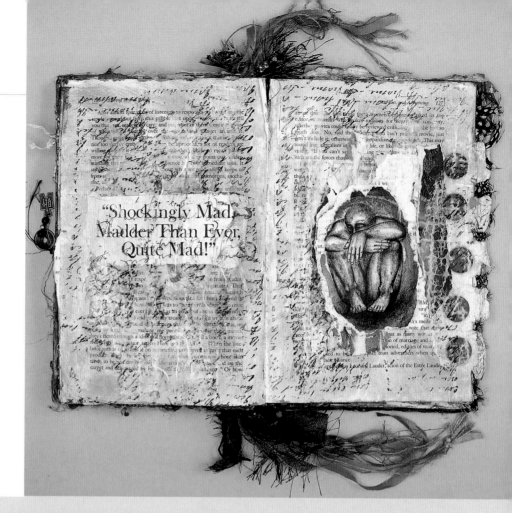

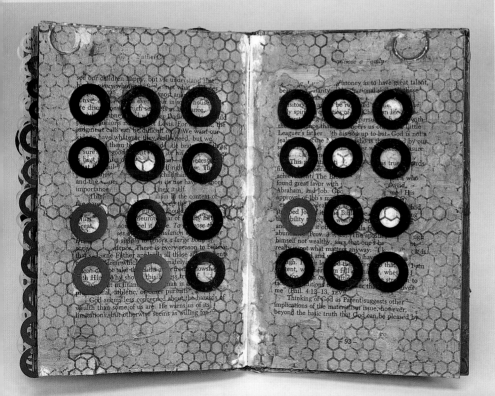

ABOVE: Even these mesh strips, though they don't have a lot of dimension, add something tangible, both to this page and to the entire book. You also can see a mesh insert that I added a few pages back and that hangs outside the perimeter of the rest of the pages.

LEFT: The washers that hang off the back of the left page provide variety. Without it, an all-washer book wouldn't be half as interesting. Again notice that when you hang embellishments outside the traditional shape of the page, these elements play a part in their own page as well as other pages and the book in general.

Adding Fibers & Beads

Fibers, beads and charms add texture and interest to altered pages. I like to lay fibers in the center of a two-page spread. It reminds me of the ribbon page markers in prayer books and hymnals. You can use any fibers, threads or strings you have laying around the house or from a craft or fabric store.

✂ MATERIALS 2 pages of your book; ⅛-inch (3mm) wide double-stick tape; assorted beads and charms; dental floss threader; three strands of fiber

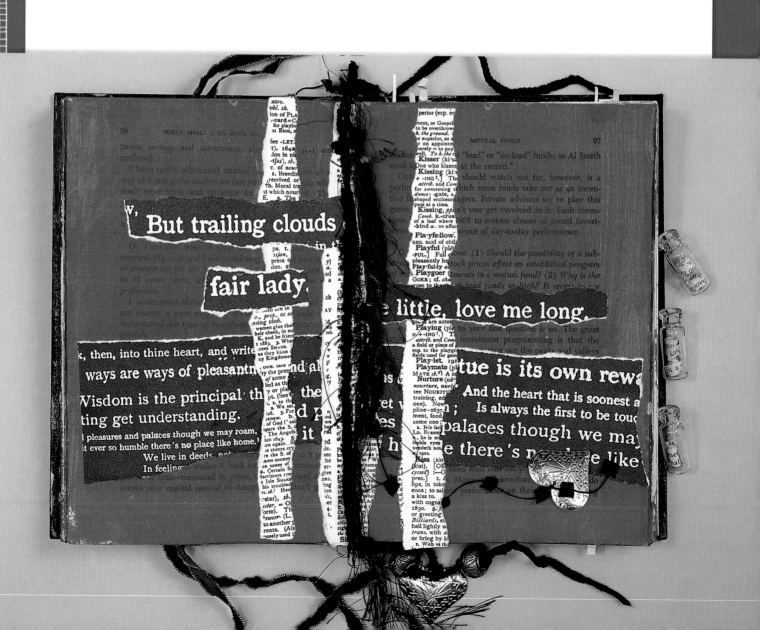

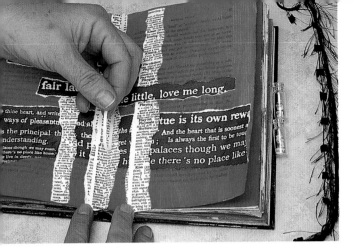

1 APPLY TAPE • Decorate a two-page spread any way you'd like. Once you're finished, apply a strip of double-stick tape from the top to the bottom of the book as close to the spine as possible. Remove the adhesive backing.

2 ADD FIBERS • Gather your strands of fiber and lay them over the tape with longer tails at the bottom than the top. I like to use fibers of various thicknesses together to add extra texture to the page. Smooth the fibers over the tape with your fingers, making sure that each strand sticks to the tape.

3 ATTACH EMBELLISHMENTS • Thread one of the strands through the dental floss threader. Then pull a charm or bead over the threader onto the fiber. Pull off the floss threader and tie a knot in the fiber to secure the charm. You can tie the knot so the bead has room to move around or you can secure it in place.

4 KEEP ADDING THEM • Add as many charms or beads as you would like. Each time, pull the fiber through the floss threader, push the embellishment over the threader onto the fiber, remove the floss threader and tie off the fiber.

TIP! If you pull a bead or charm against the grain of the fiber, the fiber will bunch. So before you put your fibers in the book, decide where you'll be hanging embellishments, and lay the fibers accordingly.

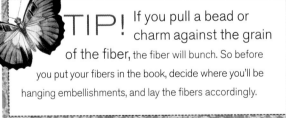

5 IMPROVE THE DESIGN • When I thought I had finished the page, I took a step back to look at it. I realized that I had added four embellishments. A standard artistic design rule is to use odd numbers of any element to add interest. So I'll add one more bead.

Variations

RIGHT: This page would just seem incomplete without a little punch of something. The fiber I added isn't even attached to the book. I just laid it in the spine. The brown part of the fiber brings out the orange in the sun on the left, and the black part of the fiber brings out the black from the figure on the right, as do the black brushstrokes scattered across the page. Fibers from other pages in the book also follow the warm color scheme established here. As a fun extra, by the way, the disk in the figure actually rotates, just like the sun!

BELOW: You got a partial view of this page when I showed you a cover variation on page 87. What looked like a simple flag through the cover of the book is a small part of a really fun design here. Plus, the back view of those bathing beauties is probably even funnier than the front. Again, without the red fibers outlining each flag shape and without the blue stars, this page would just be lacking something.

ABOVE: I created a grid pattern with these pieces of black and gold ribbon. Following a grid like this helps create a nice design. Actually outlining the grid gave the design even more impact. Hanging the ribbon from the edges of the pages created that interactive effect that makes altered books so different from traditional artwork.

LEFT: I used several different fibers with different textures here. The thickest one has a nice velvet feel, which adds a touch of class that seems worthy of the images. The fabric pattern on the background and the fibers make these powerful figures more inviting.

Transferring Images

Transferring an image gives it a transparent feel and provides a wonderful layering effect for your page. It also gives you the opportunity to use your own photography and art to personalize your pages. Here I used a photo taken by this book's photographer of her cat. I recommend making a photocopy of any image you want to transfer: You wouldn't want to permanently alter an actual photograph, of course, and two-sided images, such as those from books or magazines, don't transfer well.

✂ **MATERIALS** 2 pages in your book; flat paintbrush; gel medium; PVA glue; photocopied image enlarged or reduced to desired size; water

1 APPLY GEL MEDIUM TO THE IMAGE • Paint the two book pages any color you'd like and set the book aside to dry. Then apply at least three layers of gel medium to the front of the photocopy, letting each layer air dry before adding the next. Each layer will take at least twenty minutes to dry. The heat from a hair dryer or heat gun is probably too hot. I don't recommend them for this technique.

2 WET THE PAPER • When the gel medium is completely dry, turn the photocopy over and apply water to the back of the image with a flat brush. Use a generous amount of water and let it soak into the paper. The image will transfer into the gel medium.

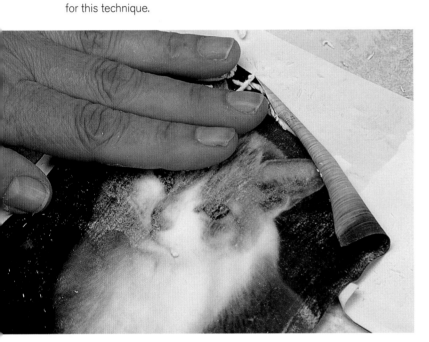

3 REMOVE THE PAPER • Gently rub the paper off the back of the gel medium until the image appears and the paper backing is gone. Start rubbing in the center of the image and work your way out to the edges; it's less likely to tear this way.

TIP! The image may appear cloudy when you first remove the paper backing. Don't worry. It will dry clear. If your image seems to tear easily as you remove the paper backing, remember this and add another coat of gel medium next time.

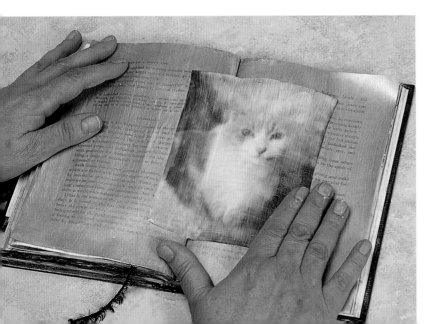

4 GLUE THE IMAGE TO THE PAGE • When the image is dry, use a flat brush to apply PVA glue to the page where you want to glue the image. Gently place the image on the glued page and smooth it out to get rid of air bubbles. Where the image overlaps the spine, push it in so the image adheres there as well. Wait for the glue to dry and decorate the page any way you'd like.

Variations

RIGHT: A transferred image can play a much more subtle and cohesive role in your design than a tangible image can. It seems to become a part of the page. In this case, three-dimensional embellishments contrast the flat image and lend the entire page more impact.

BELOW: I transferred the same image onto this page three times, something you can't do with straight collage. The buttons and cream paint add to the vintage feel. Also notice how much more unified this design feels than if I hadn't overlapped the images.

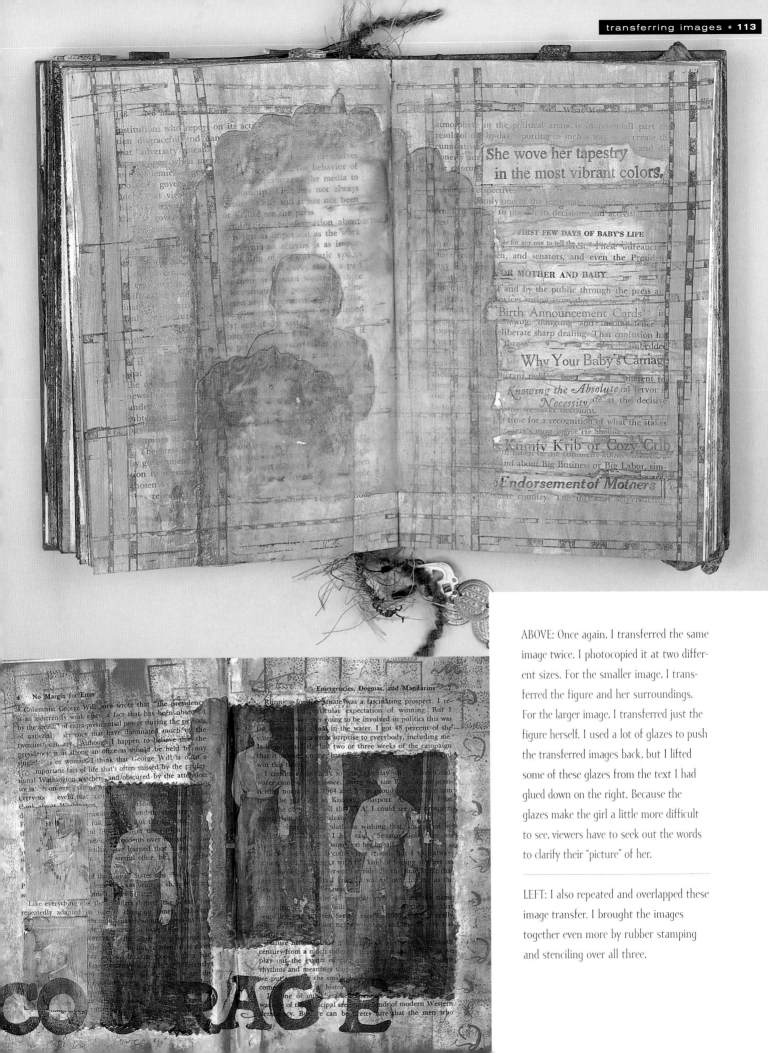

ABOVE: Once again, I transferred the same image twice. I photocopied it at two different sizes. For the smaller image, I transferred the figure and her surroundings. For the larger image, I transferred just the figure herself. I used a lot of glazes to push the transferred images back, but I lifted some of these glazes from the text I had glued down on the right. Because the glazes make the girl a little more difficult to see, viewers have to seek out the words to clarify their "picture" of her.

LEFT: I also repeated and overlapped these image transfer. I brought the images together even more by rubber stamping and stenciling over all three.

Adding Pop-Ups

I was experimenting with folding pages in a practice book one day when the idea for this pop-up page came to me. I could never figure out how children's book manufacturers made pop-ups, so I decided to simply use a page from a children's book in my own altered book. Just in time, though, this idea came to me, and now it's one of my favorites. I chose Frida Kahlo as the subject of this page, having just seen the movie *Frida*. I have always been a fan of her work. In fact, the postcard I used on this page shows her painting *Self-Portrait*.

✂ MATERIALS 4 pages in your book; alphabet tiles; 2" x 4" (5cm x 10cm) cardstock; double-stick tape; flat paintbrush; gel medium or PVA glue; inserts or tags for the pockets; pencil; postcard; purple glaze; scissors; Scotch tape

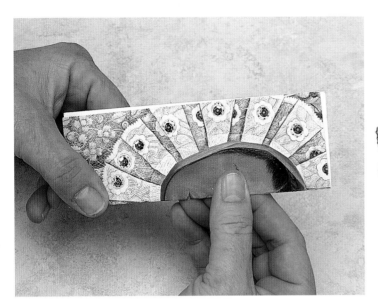

1 FOLD THE CARD • Fold a standard-size postcard in half lengthwise to form a crease.

TIP! If you want to use an image that isn't sturdy enough for a pop-up, glue the image to a piece of firm cardstock, cardboard or another postcard. You can either trim the background or leave it to serve as a mat or frame.

3 BEGIN FOLDING THE POCKETS • Fold the edge of page 2 inward toward page 3, creasing it along the margin of the text of the book page. Similarly, fold the edge of page 3 inward toward page 2, again creasing the fold along the margin.

2 POSITION THE CARD • Open the book to the back of page 2 and the front of page 3. Place the postcard over the pages, aligning the crease of your fold with the spine of the book (this guarantees that the pop-up will fold nicely when you close the book). The closer the sides of the postcard are to the spine, the higher your pop-up will sit when you open the book. On the book pages, use a pencil to mark the locations of the four corners of the postcard. You can set the card aside for now.

4 REPEAT THE FOLDS • Fold both pages in the same direction again. Fold page 2 inward toward page 3 so that the edge reaches the pencil marks on that page.

5 FINISH THE FOLDS • Fold page 3 inward toward page 2 again until the edge reaches the pencil marks on page 3. Crease both folds.

6 TAPE DOWN THE FOLDS • Unfold the last fold you made on each page. Place a piece of double-stick tape across the top and the bottom of each page, including the remaining fold. Remove the tape's adhesive backing. Redo the folds you made in steps 4 and 5, and apply pressure over the taped areas to make sure the pages are secure. You've just made a pocket from each folded page.

7 TAPE PAGE 2 • Turn to the back of page 1 and the front of page 2. Place double-stick tape across the top and bottom of the folded page and remove the adhesive backing.

8 PRESS THE PAGES TOGETHER • Press page 2 onto page 1 and burnish to make sure the tape sticks. Tape the back of page 3 to page 4 the same way. You've just created two more pockets.

9 MAKE FLAPS • Cut two pieces of cardstock that are 1 inch (3 centimeters) wide and 3½ inches (9 centimeters) long. Place the postcard on your work surface face down. Align the long edges of the cardstock and postcard. Attach each piece of cardstock to one side of the postcard with Scotch tape, leaving a gap of approximately ¹⁄₁₆ to ⅛ of an inch (2 to 3 millimeters) between them on each side.

10 TAPE THE FLAPS • Turn the postcard over again so it's facing up. Place double-stick tape along each piece of cardstock from top to bottom. Place the tape about ⅛ of an inch (3 millimeters) from the edge closest to the postcard. Remove the adhesive backing.

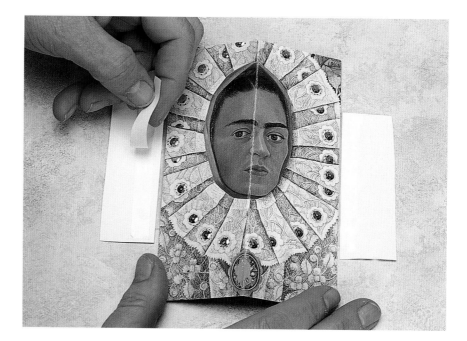

11 ATTACH THE POP-UP • Place the flaps into the pockets closest to the spine and burnish to adhere the folded pages to the double-stick tape. The flaps are hidden inside the pockets while holding the postcard in place.

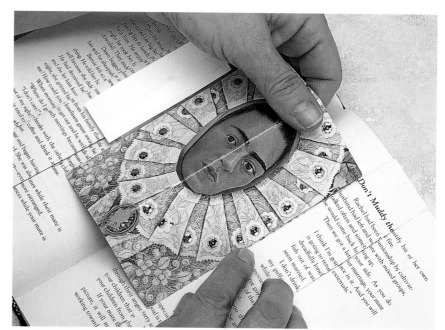

12 DECORATE THE INSERTS • You can place inserts, tags or anything else you'd like in the outer pockets. These cards add color and interest to the page. Adding one on each side keeps the design balanced and focused on the pop-up. I decided to cut the cards to the same height as the postcard for a stable, balanced feeling. Punch or decorate these inserts any way you'd like.

13 INSERT THE INSERTS •
Slide the inserts into the pockets closest
to the edges of the book.

14 DECORATE THE FOLDS •
Apply embellishments with a flat brush
and gel medium or PVA glue.

15 ADD COLOR •
Add purple glaze over the
collage image and cardstock
inserts. I added the glaze with
my finger instead of a brush to
create a bit of texture. The color
also seems to add a touch of class
and bring all of the elements together.

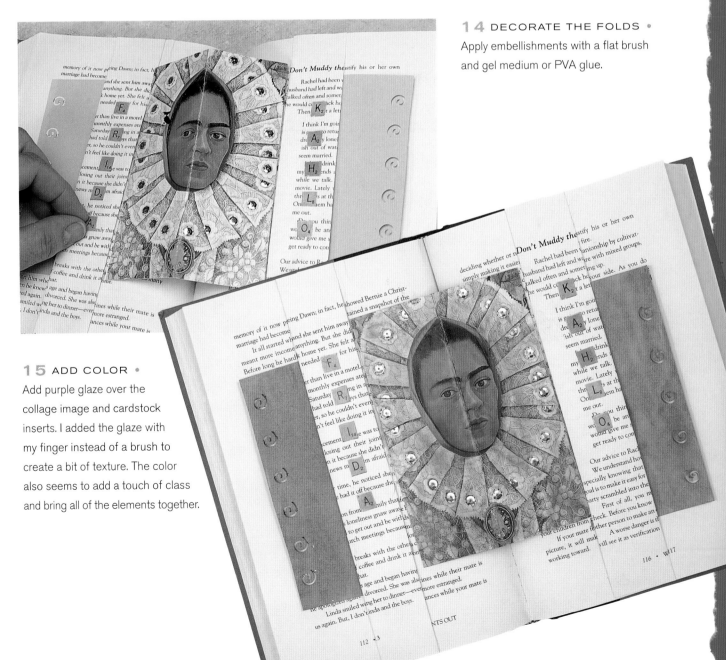

Variations

RIGHT: I love the confidence this saucy woman portrays. The way her hair pops up as one opens the book just reveals her as if she's saying, "Here I am!"

BELOW: This page is folded almost exactly the same way as the step-by-step page you just completed. But look what a difference you can make with the materials you choose. I really love the strong punch of red next to the black inserts and the white page. I tried the exact same page in another book using red pieces of round cardboard, but the matte finish just doesn't grab the viewer the same way.

LEFT: This page seems rather dismal at first. The muted background and the resigned look on this woman's face make her look pained and unhappy.

BELOW: A simple pop-up adds an entirely different meaning to the page. In the light of this inspirational quote from Winston Churchill, she still looks like someone who has been through a lot, but her expression begins to look more like determination and a will to get through it all.

We shall draw from the heart of suffering itself the means of inspiration and survival. Winston Churchill

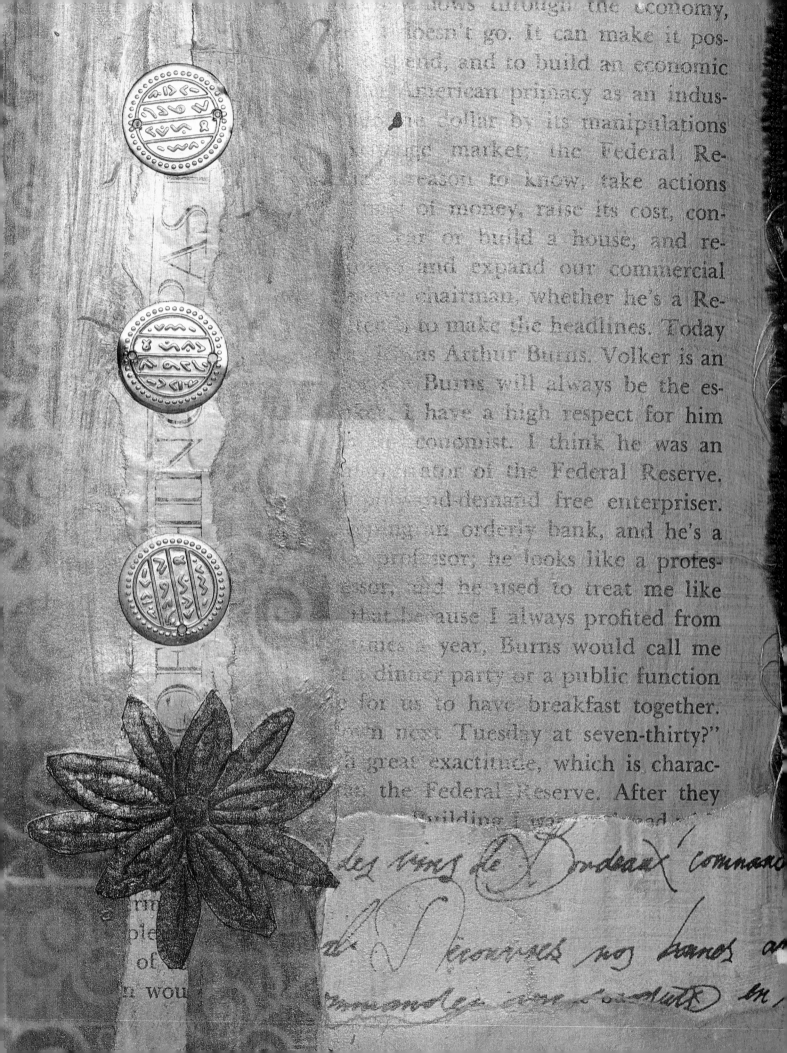

...flows through the economy,
...doesn't go. It can make it pos-
...end, and to build an economic
...American primacy as an indus-
...the dollar by its manipulations
...the market; the Federal Re-
...reason to know, take actions
...of money, raise its cost, con-
...or build a house, and re-
...and expand our commercial
...chairman, whether he's a Re-
...to make the headlines. Today
...was Arthur Burns. Volker is an
...Burns will always be the es-
...I have a high respect for him
...economist. I think he was an
...ator of the Federal Reserve.
...and-demand free enterpriser.
...an orderly bank, and he's a
...professor; he looks like a profes-
...sor, and he used to treat me like
...that because I always profited from
...a year, Burns would call me
...a dinner party or a public function
...for us to have breakfast together.
...next Tuesday at seven-thirty?"
...a great exactitude, which is charac-
...the Federal Reserve. After they
...Building I was...

les vins de Bordeaux commande

Resources

The pages in this book are composite art-works using mostly found materials from my personal collection. That's what makes the artwork my own, and using materials you collect is what will make your artwork your own.

That said, if you like the look of a certain collage paper, rubber stamp or embellishment used in this book, look it up by page number here.

Collage Papers

page 13: **PAPIER** 7 Gypsies, The Anglo Collection

page 23: **BLACK MESH** Flax art & design San Francisco

page 27: **ORNAMENT** Magenta Style, Background Papers

page 27: **LARGE SCRIPT** 7 Gypsies, The French Collection

page 30: **FRANC** 7 Gypsies, The French Collection

page 38: **ST-21** Magenta Style stickers

page 42: **SMALL SCRIPT** 7 Gypsies, The French Collection

page 42: **MILLE** 7 Gypsies, The French Collection

page 52: **LETTRES** 7 Gypsies, The Anglo Collection

page 52: **MILLE** 7 Gypsies, The French Collection

page 52: **MUSICALE** 7 Gypsies, The French Collection

page 62: **LECTURE** 7 Gypsies, The French Collection

page 62: **BORDEAUX** 7 Gypsies, The French Collection

page 78: **NUMERO** 7 Gypsies, The Anglo Collection

page 78: **SOMMES** 7 Gypsies, The French Collection

page 83: **MUSICALE** 7 Gypsies, The French Collection

page 94: **PAPIER** 7 Gypsies, The Anglo Collection

page 106: **LE MONDE** 7 Gypsies, The Anglo Collection

page 106: **NOIR** 7 Gypsies, The Anglo Collection

page 110: **SOMMES** 7 Gypsies, The French Collection

page 114: **TILES** Limited Edition Rubber Stamps

page 121: **CALLIGRAPHY** Papers by Catherine, Rossi Italian Print

Rubber Stamps

page 34: **LIFE** Judikins

page 36: **DOORS** Post Script Studio

page 47: **ARTFUL MOSAIC** Stampers Anonymous

page 47: **BREATHE** Stampers Anonymous

page 48: (A) **ASPIRE/ASTONISH** Stampers Anonymous

page 48: **ARTFUL MOSAIC** Stampers Anonymous

page 51: **RAINFOREST BUTTERFLY** Stampers Anonymous

page 51: **BUTTERFLY MEDLEY** PSX Designs for Creativity

page 55: **EVIDENCE** Stampers Anonymous

page 56: **LIFE ENERGY** Stampers Anonymous

page 56: **8507** Rubber Monger

page 56: **MASK** Stampa Barbara

page 72: **LA COLLINE VERTE** Stampers Anonymous

page 72: **PREDICT THE FUTURE** Impression Obsession

page 90: **ARTFUL MOSAIC** Stampers Anonymous

page 99: **WITH GREAT LOVE (MOTHER TERESA)** PSX Designs for Creativity

page 99: **A STAMP IN THE HAND**

page 112: **LET YOUR SPIRIT DANCE** angi-b & co

Other Supplies

page 100: **BOTTLEMANIA** American Science and Surplus

Previous Page: The collage on pages 122 and 123 used a few simple images and layers of glazes. Notice that the text of the book provides a texture to the page without taking attention away from the design I created.

Where to Find Them

If you can't find the products listed on page 124 in your local store, look here to find contact information for the manufacturers. If you need help tracking down adhesives or other general craft supplies, visit your local craft store.

Manufacturers

7 GYPSIES
4917 Genesta Ave.
Encino, CA 91316
(800) 588-6707
www.7gypsies.com

AMERICAN SCIENCE AND SURPLUS
P.O. Box 1030
Skokie, IL 60076
(847) 647-0011
www.sciplus.com

ANGI-B & CO
2418 N. 11th St.
Clinton, IA 52732
(563) 243-1151

FLAX ART & DESIGN SAN FRANCISCO
240 Valley Dr.
Brisbane, CA 94005
(800) 343-3529
www.flaxart.com

IMPRESSION OBSESSION
P.O. Box 5415
Williamsburg, VA 23188
(877) 259-0905
www.impression-obsession.com

JUDIKINS
17803 South Harvard Blvd.
Gardena, CA 90248
(310) 515-1115
www.judikins.com

LIMITED EDITION RUBBER STAMPS
1011 Bransten Rd. Ste. C
San Carlos, CA 94070
(650) 594-4242
www.limitededitionrs.com

MAGENTA STYLE
2275 Bombardier
Sainte-Julie
QC Canada J3E 2J9
(450) 922-5253
www.magentarubberstamps.com

PAPERS BY CATHERINE
11328 S. Post Oak, #108
Houston, TX 77035
(713) 723-4749
www.papersbycatherine.com

POST SCRIPT STUDIO
P.O. Box 1539
Placentia CA 92871
(714) 528-4529 (fax)
www.postscriptstudio.com

PSX DESIGNS FOR CREATIVITY
(800) 782-6748
www.psxdesign.com

RUBBER MONGER
P.O. Box 1777
Snowflake AZ 85937
(928) 536-5128
www.rubbermonger.com

STAMPA BARBARA
www.stampabarbara.com

STAMPERS ANONYMOUS
25967 Detroit Rd.
Westlake, OH 44145
(888) 326-0012
www.stampersanonymous.com

A STAMP IN THE HAND
20507 S. Belshaw Ave.
Carson, CA 90746
(310) 884-9700
www.astampinthehand.com

Swap Your Art

Round-robins, swaps, art and craft trading—it doesn't matter what you call them. They're all wonderful ways to boost your creativity, expose yourself to new and different things and just see what's out there. And the craft world hasn't been slow to pick up on that fact.

Whether you meet in person and pass a project around, mail crafts among friends across the country or trade in the online community—whether you pass one project around or trade one for another, whether you follow a predetermined theme or just make what you feel—it all achieves the same goal. It's not the making of the craft, but seeing what others are doing in their homes and studios or what you can do together that opens doors to what else is out there.

Find a Group

Look in an online community, such as WWW.GROUPS.YAHOO.COM/GROUP/ALTEREDBOOKS. There, you'll find information on art swaps and chances to participate.

Visit WWW.ALTEREDBOOKS.MEETUP.COM to meet other altered book artists in your area. Meetup.com lets you sign up for altered books—or any other craft or interest for that matter—gatherings in your area. Then the Web site will schedule an altered books meeting time across the country. Once you sign up, the site will e-mail you to let you know where the gathering will be. Or for a simpler approach, simply take out an ad in your local newspaper.

Start a Group

Convince your friends who don't have time for regular craft get-togethers to start a swap with you. You might even be able to find another group across the country with whom your group can trade collaborative projects.

Find a Swap in Progress

If being in charge just isn't your thing, look at WWW.COLLAGECAT.COM (collage swaps), WWW.20THINGS.ORG (any art or craft) or WWW.ARTISTICALLYINCLINED.CO.UK/SWAPS.HTM for swaps administered by each Web site. These are just examples, don't worry: There are plenty of them going around.

Other Fun Trades

- WWW.NERVOUSNESS.ORG, which trades any kind of art, including mixed tapes.

- WWW.FOUND-ART.COM, based on the random acts of kindness model, participants leave art in public places to be found; finders are directed to the Found Art Web site.

- WWW.SWAPPINGTONS.COM, in which you earn trading points by shipping old books, CDs or whatever you want to trade to someone who wants them; just good, old-fashioned bartering.

- WWW.1000JOURNALS.COM: 1,000 journals are traveling around the country and you can take part; a different example pops up each time you visit the site. #526 was the first to make it back home, to the site's office, by the way.

International Society of Altered Book Artists (ISABA)

The International Society of Altered Book Artists is a group of artists, hobbyists, professional artists, teachers, librarians and students who form an international, nonprofit organization dedicated to promoting book altering as an art form. Their goals:

- Educate the public about altered books

- Develop resources for altered book exhibits

- Build a traveling library of altered books, artists slides and information to mount exhibitions for galleries and institutions

- Document, compile and encourage critical writing about altered books for gallery owners, dealers and art consultants

- Develop a database of available teachers and speakers for workshops and symposiums

- Launch an annual symposium with lectures, a juried show and classes

Contact the society at:

ISABA
P.O. Box 56
Genoa, IL 60135
www.alteredbookartists.com
internationalsocietyofalteredbookartists@hotmail.com

Index

Get Creative

with North Light Books!

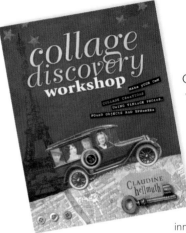

Collage Discovery Workshop

Open a new world of creativity with *Collage Discovery Workshop*. You'll learn how to create distinct collages through 12 step-by-step projects, creative exercises and journaling prompts. To enhance your pieces, you'll find 15 innovative and unique techniques for antiquing objects, transferring images and creating amazing backgrounds. Among the projects included are collaged tin refrigerator magnets, beeswax collages and shadowboxes. ISBN 1-58180-343-5, paperback, 128 pages, #32313

Vintage Greeting Cards with MaryJo McGraw

Renowned rubber stamp artist MaryJo McGraw shows you how to create unique keepsake cards featuring family photos, vintage trinkets and ephemera. Crafters of all skill levels will enjoy these distinctive ideas and papercrafting techniques, including aging paper, photo transferring and using embellishments to create 23 dazzling cards. ISBN 1-58180-413-X, paperback, 128 pages, #32583

Creative Stamping with Mixed Media Techniques

Over 20 dramatic paint and stamping recipes combine sponging, glazing and masking techniques with stamped patterns for outstanding creations. *Creative Stamping with Mixed Media Techniques* integrates traditional and nontraditional media in 13 step-by-step projects. Manipulate, decorate and combine different materials to create mixed media gifts and art objects. ISBN 1-58180-347-8, paperback, 128 pages, #32315

The Essential Guide to Making Handmade Books

Indulge your creativity! 11 projects will teach you to craft self-expressive handmade books. This guide starts with basic techniques and projects to get started and moves into more challenging bindings and formats. *The Essential Guide to Making Handmade Books* offers step-by-step instructions, visual materials lists and ideas and tips for personalizing your creation for extraordinary keepsakes and gifts. ISBN 1-58180-019-3, paperback with flaps, 128 pages, #31652

These books and other fine North Light titles are available from your local art & craft retailer, bookstore, online supplier or by calling 1-800-448-0915.